God Truly Worshipped

Jonathan Dean is a Reformation historian and Methodist minister. He read Classics at Oxford and Theology at Cambridge, where he completed a PhD supervised by Eamon Duffy. He is currently Assistant Professor of Religion at Aurora University near Chicago, and a Fellow of its Wackerlin Center for Faith and Action.

Other titles in the *Canterbury Studies in Spiritual Theology* series:

Law and Revelation: Richard Hooker and His Writings
Edited by Raymond Chapman

Heaven in Ordinary: George Herbert and His Writings
Edited by Philip Sheldrake

Before the King's Majesty: Lancelot Andrews and His Writings
Edited by Raymond Chapman

Christ Alive and At Large: The Unpublished Writings of C. F. D. Moule
Edited and introduced by Robert Morgan and Patrick Moule

Happiness and Holiness: Selected Writings by Thomas Traherne
Edited by Denise Inge

The Sacramental Life: A Gregory Dix Reader
Edited and introduced by Simon Jones

To Build God's Kingdom: F D Maurice and His Writings
Edited and introduced by Jeremy Morris

Firmly I Believe: An Oxford Movement Reader
Edited by Raymond Chapman

The Truth-Seeking Heart: An Austin Farrer Reader
Edited by Ann Loades and Robert MacSwain

God Truly Worshipped: Thomas Cranmer and His Writings
Edited by Jonathan Dean

Christ in All Things: William Temple and His Writings
Edited by Stephen Spencer

God Truly Worshipped

Thomas Cranmer and His Writings

Edited by
Jonathan Dean

CANTERBURY
PRESS
Norwich

© in this compilation Jonathan Dean 2012

First published in 2012 by the Canterbury Press Norwich
Editorial office
13–17 Long Lane,
London, EC1A 9PN, UK

Canterbury Press is an imprint of Hymns Ancient & Modern Ltd
(a registered charity)
13A Hellesdon Park Road, Norwich,
Norfolk, NR6 5DR, UK
www.canterburypress.co.uk

British Library Cataloguing in Publication data

A catalogue record for this book is available
from the British Library

978 1 84825 048 2

Originated by The Manila Typesetting Company
Printed and bound in Great Britain by
Lightning Source UK

Contents

Dedicated with gratitude to three worshipping communities:
The Chapel of Keble College, Oxford
The Cambridge Theological Federation
The Milton Keynes Mission Partnership
in which I lived, worked and prayed with Cranmer's Anglicans,
who befriended and blessed me.

Preface

I have incurred a significant number of debts in the creation of this book, and some of them are of long standing. Never far away from my thoughts is my grandfather, Eddy, whose great love for the Anglican tradition was kindled also in me when I was very young. I cherish memories of exploring Ely Cathedral, where he had been a boy chorister, with him and of discovering under his tutelage the great glories of liturgy and music to which Thomas Cranmer's church gave rise. My other grandfather, Ben, was equally well versed in the history of Tudor and Stuart England and encouraged the early delight I took in this period. I fondly remember our historical conversations even now.

The libraries in which I have pursued the documentary research have been far apart, but in each the helpfulness, courtesy and professionalism of the staff has been incomparable and invaluable. For Lambeth Palace Library in London, the Phillips Library at Aurora University and the Harold Washington and Newberry libraries in Chicago I am therefore duly grateful and to their dedicated librarians I offer my sincere thanks.

My editor at Canterbury Press, Natalie Watson, first suggested that I essay a volume in this series and then affirmed my enthusiasm to return to my Reformation roots and focus on Archbishop Cranmer. She has been tolerant of my inability to finish on time, understanding about the other commitments in my life which vied with this one, thoughtful, wise and practical with her suggestions and generous with her friendship, by which I am blessed.

It's been a privilege too to work on this project in two places: First United Methodist Church in Downers Grove, where the congregation looked with grace, kindness and enthusiasm on my ongoing research interests, and Aurora University, where I currently work and teach. In the former place, I want again to record my affection for and thanks to the staff, and especially Sharon Harman, Diane Hires, Diane Kerr and Andi Kinsella for assistance of all kinds with this and other projects.

At Aurora University, I've been fortunate in acquiring a range of supportive and thoughtful colleagues and in benefitting from a general encouragement of scholarship and enquiry. My thanks to David Fink for the helpful Reformation conversations and to good faculty colleagues for support of all kinds in the last year, and especially to Jeanine Clark Bremer, Jen Buckley, Gerald Butters, Kris Johnson, Henry Kronner, Barbara Strassberg and Jessica Thurlow. President Rebecca Sherrick's support for and affirmation of faculty research and scholarly interests deployed in the service of our students and the wider world is critical and much appreciated. Above all, I'm again indebted to my friend and colleague Martin Forward for his unflagging support for my writing career, for our enlightening chats about the Tudors in general and his insightful comments on the material itself and for countless cups of (really good) coffee along the way.

In the course of compiling and placing in context these works, I have again and again been mindful of my Anglican friends, who have, over the years, enabled this low-church Methodist better to appreciate the beauty and depth of their tradition. As a child, I was lucky that our dear family friends, the Shirleys, holidayed with us. The 'ABC' tours which Anne and my mother instituted on these occasions were of inestimable delight and benefit to me: although I think not viewed quite so enthusiastically by all the children in our party. Still, I at least am grateful: to Anne, for guided ecclesiastical tours sometimes conducted in the face of the disapproval of the official cathedral volunteers; and to Tony who, though not born an Anglican, nevertheless ensured that appropriate refreshment concluded such excursions and whose presence with us is still much missed. Graham Finch nobly fostered my interest by devoting a week to showing the sixteen-year-old me around the greater churches of South-West England and has remained a dear friend ever since. I am the richer for conversations with and the friendship of Dr Fraser Watts, whose attractive and compelling understanding of the potential of Anglicanism's gifts for modernity has always inspired me. Bishop Geoffrey Rowell was a model college chaplain and continues to be a mentor and valued counsellor across denominational divides. My friends Peter Baugh, Karen Turner, Justin White and William Parry have similarly educated and helped me. Twenty years after we met and became friends, I'm especially grateful for William's continued presence in my life.

Other friends again endured my creative angst and absorption with a dead clergyman, offering unstinting support in all kinds of ways. I'm gifted with the friendship of other Brits-in-exile here and wish to thank Ray and Ina Osborn for their care and love. For them too, especially as former Anglicans, the sound of Cranmerian prose stirs a measure of homesickness and nostalgia; and it's good to find people who share one's pain while also sharing their wine. In addition, I am thankful to my generous clergy friends in Chicago, to my wonderful sister, Louise, to my dear parents Joy and Richard and to Trey Hall for all their extraordinary and unconditional love and encouragement. My dog Jake has been immeasurably helpful by insisting that I take regular breaks from the laptop for walks along the river.

Religious faith and a better understanding of the faith of others is really only formed in community, through friendship and dialogue. And so, I want to offer this book as a tribute to three communities of faith in which I learned about and was utterly captivated by the Anglican tradition. In the chapel of Keble College, Oxford, as a student and then lecturer at Wesley House, Cambridge (where for a year my room overlooked the Fellows' garden at Jesus College, in which Cranmer once walked) and therefore of the interdenominational Cambridge Theological Federation and as a minister in the Milton Keynes Mission Partnership, Anglican friends and colleagues have shaped and informed my life and changed it for the better. This book is in part a fruit of those relationships. To these places of work, worship and exploration it is therefore offered, with affectionate gratitude.

A note on text transcriptions: I have modernized the spelling of Cranmer's works for the ease of modern readers; but retained his original punctuation and capitalization. They can seem eccentric: but I hope this preserves at least a measure of authenticity.

Introduction

Our eyes are blinded by the holiness you bear.
The bishop's robe, the mitre and the cross of gold
Obscure the simple man within the Saint.
Strip off your glory . . . and speak![1]

Thomas Cranmer was not one of the Reformation's great original thinkers or theologians. He did not, as Martin Luther, unleash the energies of a whole generation in a monumental movement of religious change. He was no John Calvin, defining the contours of reformed theology and practice through a massive and meticulous systematic exposition intended for the guidance of future generations. Nor was he even an Ulrich Zwingli, reimagining the Eucharist in controversial and dynamic fashion. For all that, a claim of a different kind may be made for Cranmer. If not the most original, brilliant or critical leader of the varied Reformation movements of the sixteenth century, his work is by far the most influential in the lives of the ordinary Christians he so cared about, and it has enjoyed a much greater longevity. It was given to him, for six extraordinary years half way through that turbulent century, dramatically to renew English Christianity. And his most significant achievement in those years, the *Book of Common Prayer*, is perhaps the most widely read and massively influential publication of the entire Reformation. Long after anyone except theologians and church historians ceased to care about Luther's *Babylonian Captivity of the Church* or Calvin's *Institutes*, millions of people across the globe are still understanding and articulating their lives' most significant moments and experiences by means of his prose. Generations after the bitter debates and disputes of the era, which now seem backward and unenlightened, Cranmer's language still gives expression to the prayers of the English-speaking world. There is perhaps no greater testament to this quiet, scholarly, gentle, committed yet compassionate man than the universal appeal which his elegant, intuitively insightful liturgy now exercises

---

1 Eric Crozier, *Saint Nicolas*, opening.

I

among Christians, of all shades and kinds. It is the kind of mass, far-reaching appeal of which his peers could only dream.

So, who was this man, the work of whose life still undergirds our worship and the manner of whose death still inspires claims to sainthood, an icon of faithfulness and courage in an age of change, brutality and violence? In fact, he was not someone obviously marked for greatness. Born to relatively humble parentage in the small Nottinghamshire village of Aslockton in 1489, Cranmer spent two-thirds of his life in virtual obscurity, first at home and school and then, for almost thirty years, as scholar and teacher in Cambridge, a Fellow of Jesus College. His father, the elder Thomas, had made sure before his death in 1501 to make provision for his sons' education, and Thomas the younger arrived at his new college in 1503, to study divinity.

Even in Cambridge, little is known of Cranmer's life. Evidence survives of his commitment to traditional forms of religion in the early sixteenth century and therefore to the papacy as the only sure guarantor of Christian unity and authenticity, binding the world together in shared authority, insight and practice. Evidence survives too that his scholarship was rooted in the humanism of the day: Cranmer shared the world-view of such luminaries as Desiderius Erasmus, John Fisher and Thomas More that a return to original sources, read in their original languages, was crucial in the study of theology as much as in any other area. This scholarly method was revolutionizing European thought, and during Cranmer's formative years in Cambridge was slowly beginning to push a young man named Martin Luther, Cranmer's elder by six years, towards startling new discoveries.

We know too that the young Fellow of Jesus was the marrying kind. Sometime before his twentieth birthday, he took a wife, Joan. The union meant the loss of his Fellowship,[2] and Cranmer found a job lower down the academic hierarchy at Buckingham College, later to be refounded as Magdalene. The marriage soon ended in tragedy, when Joan died delivering their first child, who also perished. The one mercy for Cranmer in what must have been his utter desolation was that he was re-admitted to his post at Jesus College and resumed his duties there. The circumstances of his first marriage were sometimes raised and insultingly

---

2 Fellows of both Cambridge and Oxford colleges were required to be celibate. The rule persisted for many years; John Wesley even in 1751 forfeited his Fellowship of Lincoln College, Oxford, on his marriage to Molly Vazeille.

questioned during Cranmer's final months, but he remained silent on the period ever after. In 1532, on the eve of his sudden and dramatic appointment as Archbishop of Canterbury, he married again: Margarete, the niece of the prominent reformer Andreas Osiander of Nuremburg. By this time, he was an ordained priest, which made the match more risky. Indeed, a world of change and turmoil separated the two marriages, and by the second Cranmer's views on papal authority were evidently changing and he was about to be stunned by the offer of the highest ecclesiastical office in England.

During the early 1520s, though, we must suppose that the young widower spent his days in study, teaching and in the company of other Cambridge men. We have some small glimpses of Cranmer as teacher, for instance a passage in his *Answer* to Gardiner from 1551, in which he dismisses his opponent by likening him to lazy Cambridge students 30 years earlier, who pretended to have done the reading for their tutorial when in fact they had not and who had to be given a dressing-down by their instructor.[3] Other than this kind of colourful anecdote, we know little of these years, except that Cranmer looked back on them fondly: as a time when he had greater leisure to enjoy his books, a time when no affairs of state pressed on him and as a period when, without the huge attendant costs and duties of being the Primate of All England, he was comparatively rather better off.

In the mid-1520s, Cranmer caught the eye of the powerful Cardinal Thomas Wolsey, Archbishop of York, Lord Chancellor and the King's chief minister, mover and arranger of the state's affairs. Wolsey was always on the look out for talented young scholars who might be useful members of the diplomatic corps, and Cranmer fitted the bill. It was the beginning of a move away from the cloistered seclusion of Cambridge and towards the high politics of Henrician England and its relations with continental Europe. Those very relations, of course, were about to be put under intolerable strain by the King's evolving sense that he was married to the Queen in a manner offensive to God and normal decency. She was Catherine, daughter of King Ferdinand II of Aragon and Queen Isabella I of Castile and, more to the point, the widow of Henry's elder brother Prince Arthur. Henry had taken his sister-in-law as his own bride after his accession in 1509 and after a long wrangle to

---

3 Thomas Cranmer, *The works of Thomas Cranmer, Archbishop of Canterbury, Martyr 1556*, 2 vols, ed. John Edmund Cox (Cambridge: Parker Society, 1844–6), vol. 1, *Writings and disputations, relative to the sacrament of the Lord's Supper*, p. 305.

obtain the necessary papal dispensation for such a union. A combination of factors prompted Henry's scruples, after 15 years or so; the two most powerful of which were the lack of a male heir and the presence at court of a young girl the King found utterly bewitching and beguiling, one Anne Boleyn.

Cranmer, in the service of Cardinal Wolsey, soon found himself embroiled in the increasingly desperate quest to find a way to obtain the Pope's permission for the Aragon marriage to be annulled. His real contribution to the effort was not especially creative, but seemed at the time like a vital fresh approach. Over dinner with other young diplomats, including his soon-to-be arch-rival Stephen Gardiner, he casually suggested that the universities of Europe should be more assiduously canvassed for their views on the King's 'Great Matter', as a means to strengthen their case and to force the Pope's hand. The contribution was taken up with alacrity; Cranmer was summoned to London for meetings with Wolsey and even the King and was sent on further embassies overseas in this cause. Cranmer, more than ever, had propelled himself with characteristic humility and without any apparent plan or intention to do so into the front rank of Henry's retinue.

One of the reasons why Thomas Cranmer is such an absorbing and fascinating figure is that he embodies rather strikingly the historical truth that those whose convictions shape events have always come to those convictions over a period of time. They do not emerge from the womb holding all the views for which they will later be known. Cranmer's intellectual development is especially interesting. The first stage of his odyssey he held in common with many of his peers, including those who would later fiercely oppose his innovations in the English Church. He came to subscribe, at exactly what point we cannot tell, to the central idea by means of which Henry finally got his divorce, that of the royal supremacy. In other words, Cranmer came to share with Henry and his councillors the belief that it was the King, by virtue of his royal status, whom God regarded as the head of the Church in his own kingdom. The claims of the Bishops of Rome, therefore, were bogus and dangerous and had always been so. Henry, next under God, ruled the English Church as much as he ruled any other part or parcel of his realm. If we are to understand Cranmer and his life's work, we must understand this world-view, however odd it now sounds to modern ears.

It was to this understanding that English policy, expressing the mind of the King, moved in the early 1530s. For Cranmer, the prevailing shift in the mood was perhaps bolstered by his experiences of meeting continental Reformers in person and spending time with them, seeing the effects of religious change in their cities and engaging with them in scholarly discussion, something he always relished. He would also have appreciated the careful, humanist methods which Henry's thinkers used in arriving at and then claiming authority for their doctrine, based on ancient authors and records and presented in methodical detail. We should be careful, especially in Cranmer's case, not to see this as mere expediency or a careless shifting of position. Once he accepted the theological and historical truth of the supremacy, he built his whole life upon it and literally gave his life to it. Indeed, be became increasingly disturbed about what his loyalty to Queen Mary entailed, who had, he believed, inherited the royal supremacy despite her fervent desire to reunite England to the papacy; this confusion was a major cause of his mental anguish in the last weeks of his life. Under Henry and Edward, however, the supremacy was the vital theological foundation upon which Cranmer set about the English Reformation.

For Cranmer, at least, a conviction about the royal supremacy was also coupled with an emergent evangelicalism. That is to say, he began increasingly to espouse some of the central tenets of the Protestant Reformation, especially in believing that a greater centrality of authority and prominence of place needed to be given to the Bible in determining the Church's life and practice. Rescuing and restoring the place of the Bible in English Christian life, in fact, became the other great focus of his career, along with the fashioning of a genuinely English liturgy. In this, he became a follower of Martin Luther and was articulating the one central belief which spanned all the Reformation's disagreements and divisions. He held passionately that the one sure cure for the corruption and evils besetting the Church was to return, in a humanist manner, to sources, and especially to the Source: Scripture itself, and Scripture alone. These were the evolutions in Cranmer's thinking taking place through the late 1520s and 1530s, and these convictions placed him among the evangelical party by the time he had established himself as an ambassador of the King. In particular, he was close to the wealthy and influential Boleyn family, whose head, Thomas, was carefully cementing his family's place in the King's favour and his daughter's in the King's heart. For those like Stephen Gardiner, who firmly espoused the royal supremacy while still fiercely resisting any and all manifestations of Protestant thought in England, the influence of Cranmer and the Boleyns represented a threat to orthodoxy and a challenge to centuries of religious tradition.

Cranmer's successful prosecution of his mission in Europe soon won him favour and reward. He was given the living of Bredon in

Worcestershire, though he seems unlikely to have spent much time there and then, when Gardiner was made Bishop of Winchester, the archdeaconry of Taunton. Gardiner's promotion was spectacular, but was soon to be eclipsed by that of Cranmer himself. The aged Archbishop William Warham died in August 1532 after a long and sometimes bitter career, and the King swiftly nominated the young Cambridge man to succeed him. Everyone, not least Cranmer himself, seems to have been stunned at the nomination of someone who had exercised no real ecclesiastical office. The papal approval for the prestigious appointment was duly received, and Cranmer returned home to England as Archbishop-elect.

As we have seen, however, he returned home with something rather unusual for someone in his position: a wife. It is the clearest sign we have of Cranmer's new commitments at the time of his election. Marriage, as a priest, had been a very courageous enterprise and displayed his evangelical convictions boldly, perhaps even rashly. Returning to Henrician England and the ban on clerical marriage which persisted for the rest of the King's life, Thomas and especially Margarete Cranmer took on the necessity of a closeted existence which must have brought them great tension and fear, particularly at those moments when the conservative forces surrounding the King most had the Archbishop in their sights. We can only imagine the pressure this placed them under, but we may also imagine how critical this relationship was to the man who later wrote so eloquently of the 'mutual society, help, and comfort' that husbands and wives enjoyed in marriage.

Once installed in Canterbury and in his several palaces throughout the South East, the new Archbishop moved swiftly and with conviction to grant the King what he had so desperately desired for so long. Acting unilaterally and in a way sure to draw down the anger of Rome, Cranmer convened a trial in the priory at Dunstable, close to Queen Catherine's lodging, to give final judgement on the divorce. Catherine, predictably but very helpfully for Cranmer's cause, refused to acknowledge the court's authority and renewed her perpetual appeal to Rome. On 23 May 1533 Cranmer ruled the Aragon marriage invalid. Five days later, he validated Henry's marriage to Anne Boleyn, which he himself had not conducted. The Queen retreated in despair, but refused to recognize the decision's validity or her young successor as queen. Henry therefore continued to treat her and their daughter Mary callously, seeing their failure to accept the verdict of the court as a personal slight; Cranmer's complicity in this cruelty was a contributing factor in Mary's own anger against him when she took the throne 20 years later. Catherine died in 1536, protesting to the end her love for the King and her status as his wife. Mary was not allowed to see her, nor to attend her funeral in Peterborough Cathedral.

The divorce by no means initiated the split from Rome and England's rejection of the Pope's authority in church affairs, but it did mark something of a watershed, the final thumbing of the nose perhaps at an institution that had denied the King his wishes so stubbornly. In fact, through a series of pieces of legislation the country had been slowly sloughing off its loyalties to the Pope for a number of years, most notably as the clergy were forced to submit to the King's authority. Now, after the Dunstable determination, momentum was gained. Government declarations through the rest of 1533 attacked the Pope more forcefully; in 1534, through another series of legislative acts, England broke all ties with and all loyalty towards the Bishops of Rome and asserted its ecclesiastical independence, under the King's headship and the oversight of a General Council of the whole Church. In addition, an Act of Supremacy, enforced with an oath to be taken by all, declared that Anne was now queen, and her offspring Henry's rightful heirs. Cranmer began to ordain bishops for the English Church, another sign that Henry was now firmly in charge of religious matters in his own realm.

In all of this, of course, agonizing conflicts of loyalty, conviction and conscience were stirred up. Most famously, Bishop John Fisher of Rochester and the Lord Chancellor, Sir Thomas More, found themselves isolated, opposed to Catherine's humiliating rejection, convinced that the papacy was the only guarantor of Christian unity and therefore sick at heart as events unfolded. Many indeed found themselves similarly in turmoil and doubt, and Cranmer soon bore some of the weight of ensuring that the divorce and the disavowal of obedience to the Pope it represented were accepted by all. He was required to interview Elizabeth Barton, the 'Maid of Kent', whose mystical pronouncements against the divorce had been a real source of anxiety for the regime and then to play a role in her condemnation; and he was among those who met with More in the final months of his life, pleading with him to submit even while realizing that he could not and would not. Cranmer characteristically seems to have tried to find a way out for this great scholar and statesman and then to soften the blow as it became inevitable that it would fall. But it was all in vain. Twenty years later, the preacher at Cranmer's final trial cited the execution of Bishop Fisher as the reason Cranmer's own death was now required; for all that, he seems to have been possessed of a very clear sense about the divorce and the repudiation of papal authority, that he could do no other.

Life as the King's faithful servant soon caught Cranmer up, too, in the maelstrom of the court. The Archbishop had the advantage of being able legitimately to be in his diocese for long periods of time and regularly availed himself of the privilege. For all that, being one of Henry VIII's closest advisors and confidants, not to mention one trusted by the King with the execution of policy, was rarely a comfortable or secure kind of existence. Cranmer had witnessed the spectacular falls of Wolsey and More and must soon have realized the precarious position occupied by all on whom Henry relied. He was not alone: apart from himself, the great winner in the affair of the divorce and the separation from Rome was Thomas Cromwell, whose power increased through the 1530s and whose influence was for a time absolute. Indeed, Cromwell, who was not ordained, was invested in 1535 with the odd title of the King's 'vicegerent in spirituals', furnishing him with ultimate authority even in church matters. Cranmer was largely uninvolved in, though supportive of, the dissolution of England's ancient monastic institutions which Cromwell effected using these extraordinary powers. A sign of his genuine humility, Cranmer seems not even to have minded losing this pre-eminence to a layman, nor to have objected when the King redistributed large amounts of the lands belonging to the archbishopric to benefit Cromwell. As he said himself:

> For I pray God never be merciful unto me at the general judgement, if I perceive in my heart that I set more by any title, name, or style that I write, than I do by the paring of an apple, farther than it shall be to the setting forth of God's word and will.[4]

Unlike many of his colleagues and rivals, Cranmer seems to have remained largely above the rough and tumble of much court politics. Nevertheless, his intercessions for those he loved and admired, Thomas Cromwell and Anne Boleyn among them, exhibit great compassion and greater courage, despite the later criticisms some have offered of his timidity in public life, and will be examined later.[5] Unlike many around him too, including Cromwell, Cranmer was not hungry for

---

4 From a letter to Cromwell answering an opportunistic charge from Stephen Gardiner that his ancient title of 'Primate of all England' was an affront to the royal supremacy; quoted in Diarmaid MacCulloch, *Thomas Cranmer* (New Haven and London: Yale University Press, 1996), p. 132.

5 For instance, his very eminent successor in Saint Augustine's throne, Michael Ramsey: in Ramsey et al. (eds), *The English Prayer Book, 1549–1662* (London: SPCK, 1963), p. 1; for his letters, see Chapter 1 below.

further personal preferment or influence with the King, beyond what was necessary for the godly reformation of the English Church as he saw it. Even so, he proved a frequent target as others jostled for power and became frustrated with their own position and with that of those closer to Henry. Even Cromwell, it seems, had cause on occasion to criticize the Archbishop to the King; but all to no avail. Ralph Morice, Cranmer's secretary, overheard Cromwell in a moment of expansive dinner conversation, remark to Cranmer:

> You my Lord were born in an happy hour I suppose; for do or say what you will, the King will always take it well at your hand. And I must needs confess, that in some things I have complained of you to his Majesty, but all in vain, for he will never give credit against you, whatsoever is laid to your charge: but let me, or any other of the Council, be complained of, his Grace will most seriously chide, and fall out with us; and therefore you are most happy, if you can keep you in this state.[6]

Cranmer had got Henry his divorce, and Cranmer had implemented the King's supremacy. For these cherished achievements, and because of the deep personal connection and even pastoral dependence that the King felt towards him, Cranmer was safe and thus also a rarity in the Henrician court.

Only once was Thomas Cranmer's position genuinely and seriously threatened, during the so-called 'Prebendaries' Plot' of 1543. This was in fact a coalition of Kentish gentry, senior clergy and other prominent traditionalists intent on a 'decapitation' strategy (perhaps quite literally) against English evangelicalism by removing the Archbishop himself. At its centre was Bishop Stephen Gardiner, at the height of his conservative influence in religious matters. Cranmer was saved by what MacCulloch calls his 'unheroic obedience' in recently having promulgated religious changes of which he himself disapproved and by the same affection of the King already noted. Months after Cranmer's detractors had given the King a dossier outlining the Archbishop's heretical views and behaviour, at a time when other prominent evangelicals had been brought down and in an atmosphere of increasing danger for them, the King came down on Cranmer's side. Henry passed on the dossier to his Archbishop and placed its main target in charge of an investigation

---

6 J. G. Nichols (ed.) *Narratives of the Reformation* (London: Camden Society, 1859), pp. 259–9, referred to in MacCulloch, *Thomas Cranmer*, p. 252.

into its truth. At a subsequent meeting of the Council, Cranmer put his enemies to flight by producing the King's own ring, given to him as a sign of trust and favour. Strype reports Henry saying to Cranmer after that meeting:

> I would you should well understand, that I account my Lord of Canterbury as faithful a man towards me as ever was prelate in this realm, and one to whom I am many ways beholden, by the faith I owe to God. And therefore who loveth me will upon that account regard him.[7]

The story well illustrates, however, the kind of back-and-forth which official policy experienced under Henry, not least in religious affairs. Throughout, as we shall see, Cranmer's passion and purpose focused on ensuring that as many English people as possible were able to 'read, mark and inwardly digest' the words of Scripture, on creating a new English liturgy and on cleansing the English Church of any elements of belief or practice which he felt were incompatible with the Bible's teaching.[8] At various times, he underwent significant setbacks to these goals. The demise of Anne Boleyn in 1536 and then of Thomas Cromwell in 1540 dealt severe blows to evangelical influence; the promulgation of the Six Articles in 1539 reversed many of the more Protestant declarations of the Ten Articles three years earlier, rejecting the idea that justification came through faith alone and reinstituting mandatory clerical celibacy: which forced Cranmer to send his wife and children overseas for safety and Hugh Latimer to resign his bishopric; the *King's Book* in 1543 restated more conservative views in opposition to the gently reforming *Bishops' Book* of 1537. Hardest of all for Cranmer to bear, access to the Bible was also restricted by law under this conservative backlash in the early 1540s. Cranmer chose to set aside his own objections and obey, trusting that in due time the pendulum would swing again and his own freedom to implement change would be greater. For this, many have criticized him as cowardly and lacking in purpose; he was, however, capable of great courage when he judged the occasion demanded it. His sense of the *realpolitik* may disappoint those wanting him to have behaved with greater zeal and commitment, but this overlooks the rashness which such a course of action would have entailed.

---

7 For a full account of the 1543 plot, see MacCulloch, *Thomas Cranmer*, pp. 295–323.

8 See below, Chapter 2.

In addition, we should remember that, even and especially late in King Henry's reign, in the face of significant opposition within the court and beyond, Cranmer's achievements in the cause of reform were real and hard-won: the ending of the veneration of relics, the outlawing of indulgences and the abolition of old forms of veneration which he believed to be mere superstition.[9] It should also be noted that his patience was eventually rewarded, with the six years of Edward's reign in which progress towards a reformed Church of England under his now unrestricted leadership became swift and sure.

By the time of Henry's death in January 1547, momentum was indeed with Cranmer's party again: the Council appointed to assume control during the minority of the young Prince Edward was decidedly evangelical, and some have even suggested that the King was about to abolish Mass and the insistence on clerical celibacy.[10] Be that as it may, the Archbishop's own place in the King's affections and emotional world was certain and assured. There had been difficult moments: besides Cranmer's pleas for the innocence of Anne Boleyn and Thomas Cromwell, he had also been the only one of the Council brave enough to inform the King late in 1541 of the serial indiscretions and infidelities of Queen Catherine Howard, a most unpleasant and unnerving task.[11] He had earned the King's trust and love, however, and as Henry lay dying his only wish was to have his Archbishop by his side. Cranmer eased the passage from this world of this brilliant and yet psychologically flawed and extraordinarily difficult man, holding his hand and offering him the consolations of faith. He must have known as he did so that unparallelled possibilities were about to open up for the English Church; and he must already have been praying for the new King to live a long life, so that religious changes might take root.

The character of Cranmer's remarkable achievements under Edward VI are the focus of later chapters and need not be dwelt on too much here. From the beginning of the reign, there was a clear and intentional policy of reform, but one which was carefully calculated to proceed with care and without upsetting too many apple carts or ingrained English sensibilities. Cranmer feared that a headlong rush towards reform would provoke accusations that he and the Council were manipulating

---

9 See, among others, Eamon Duffy, *The Stripping of the Altars* (New Haven and London: Yale University Press, 1992), pp. 424–47.

10 A claim made by John Foxe and repeated by Diarmaid MacCulloch: *Tudor Church Militant* (London: Penguin, 1999), p. 58.

11 Characteristically, Cranmer also then became confessor and counsellor to the Queen, an act of great mercy and kindness; see below, Chapter 1.

an infant king and so exercised a shrewd mixture of caution and zeal.[12] Indeed, this 'gradualism in the service of calculated destruction'[13] should not mask the real urgency which underlay the Council's work, as Cranmer's address at Edward's coronation had demonstrated. The goal was a uniformity of reformed Christian expression throughout the kingdom. In the summer of 1547, preaching was the focus as licences became harder to come by and a set of official homilies was published and prescribed for parish use; Bishops Bonner and Gardiner were imprisoned for protesting against the direction of policy; and the path to further reform was clear. Communion in both kinds – that is, the distribution of bread *and* wine to worshippers, a major contention of the continental Reformation – was authorized, and Cranmer set his team to work on producing an English liturgy for the English people. In 1548, a new catechism appeared, although its Lutheran views of the Communion later proved something of a headache for Cranmer. Finally, in 1549, a publishing sensation: the first edition of the *Book of Common Prayer*, the first step towards the revolution in English worship that the Archbishop intended. It swept away at a stroke centuries of belief and practice, translating some ancient texts into perfectly polished English versions and entirely replacing others with exquisite new forms and patterns.

Progress towards the kind of English Church Cranmer envisaged picked up speed in the early 1550s as the reforming cause took root. Growing in influence and authority, he worked to place supporters in key bishoprics around the country. He brought over from the continent some of the key minds of the European Reformation to assist him, setting them up in positions of influence where they might help direct the course of the Reformation in England: Peter Martyr Vermigli, the Italian-born theologian, came to the Regius Professorship at Oxford, and Martin Bucer left Strasbourg to take a chair in Divinity at Cambridge. Paul Fagius, also in Strasbourg, joined Bucer as the Professor of Hebrew. Jan Łaski travelled from Poland via Emden to pastor the Stranger Church in London, a refuge for Protestants fleeing persecution in Europe; he also exercised influence on the direction of events in the Church of England. Bernardino Ochino made his way to a position at Canterbury and a stipend from the King, where he wrote theological treatises and became another valued adviser to the Archbishop. Cranmer indeed placed the utmost value on these connections and this kind

---

12 Duffy, *Stripping of the Altars*, p. 448.
13 MacCulloch, *Tudor Church Militant*, p. 74.

of interaction between England and the continental Reformers. He had ambitious dreams, as several formerly Protestant strongholds fell to the Catholic fightback, of using England's relative stability to make it the focus and centre of the ongoing Reformation. He envisioned a grand Europe-wide council of Protestant leaders to rival the Catholic renewal under way at the Council of Trent and vigorously lobbied the doyens of the movement, Philipp Melanchthon and John Calvin, to secure their participation. Calvin was cool; but, had Edward lived longer, Cranmer might have had his wish; he certainly lacked nothing in energy or strength of purpose.

The prayer book of 1549 was always in Cranmer's eyes merely a stopgap, designed to begin a process of change and not to be its last word. As he expressed himself, writing in 1551, the removal of Catholic theology was always going to be a more delicate process than the mere denial of papal supremacy:

> The Bishop of Rome was not clean gone out of England, as soon as the laws were made against his authority.[14]

In 1552, he produced the second edition. As examined in Chapter 4, it represented a further revolution in the theology of the English Church. Most notably, it reflected the final stage of Cranmer's own theological odyssey, espousing an understanding of Holy Communion which closely resembled the mainstream of European Reformation thought. This had been an even longer evolution for him than his views on ecclesiastical governance; and one rather harder definitively to chart. Piecing together the official documents themselves and the rare moments when Cranmer talks autobiographically, it is possible to offer some sort of timeline.

Martin Luther had criticized much of the medieval practice of the Eucharist, including the belief that the Mass was itself a 'sacrifice' and the practice of priests offering solitary Masses for the dead in purgatory. But he had always maintained a sense of the 'real presence': that, after the prayer of consecration, the body and blood of Christ were physically present. He toned down the traditional understanding of the complete transformation of bread and wine into Christ's body and blood ('transubstantiation'), however, by suggesting that bread and wine remained *along with* the new presence of Christ's flesh and blood. Cranmer seems to have embraced this Lutheran view by the

---

14 In his *Answer* to Gardiner: Cranmer, *Writings and Disputations*, p. 240.

early 1530s, and some of Henry's more stringently conservative pronouncements on the Eucharist, for instance in the Six Articles, pushed the Archbishop to the edge of what he could tolerate: and even perhaps beyond, although he maintained his usual outward loyalty. Towards the end of Henry's life, Cranmer's views were evolving again, away from any notion of a 'real' presence and towards a sense that what happened in the receiving of Communion was a purely spiritual event. It is important to remember that the leading Reformers could not agree on exactly what this meant or what was 'happening' at the Communion table. Cranmer, influenced especially by his friendships with Bucer and Heinrich Bullinger in Zurich, eventually concluded that, as the believer consumed the elements in faith, God imparted spiritual nourishment and sustenance which confirmed and formed Christians in their identity and within the body of Christ. There were several strands to this belief for him, among them the idea that Christ's body, once ascended, was now only in heaven and a conviction, common to all the major Reformers, that only those predestined for salvation could find the Eucharist effectual. By 1552, Cranmer was thus a thoroughgoing exponent of the doctrine often misleadingly called 'Calvinism': that God had already created an 'elect', privileged to be redeemed from sin and spend eternity in heaven.[15] Only with care and by making haste slowly did Cranmer enshrine these understandings as the doctrine of the Church in England. The second Prayer Book and the Forty-Two Articles of 1553 ensured that they were reflected in liturgy and official statements of belief. Images were whitewashed from church walls: the rood screens that divided nave from chancel and reminded medieval Catholics of the sacrifice of Christ renewed in the Mass were destroyed; altars were dismantled and replaced with simple Communion tables for the reception of bread and wine; lay people found the theatrical spectacle of the Mass replaced with a simple meal; the abiding medieval concern for the place and welfare of the dead was overcome with an increasing emphasis on the right faith and proper Christian practice of the living.

There was opposition and disruption too. The King's uncle and Lord Protector, Edward Seymour, Duke of Somerset, soon alarmed his fellow councillors with his ambition and thirst for power; after being removed from the Protectorship in 1549, he was finally executed in 1552 for scheming against his successor, John Dudley, Duke of Northumberland.

---

15 It was a theology to which Luther, Zwingli, Calvin and all the major Reformers subscribed, based on a close – and rather uncritical – reading of Augustine of Hippo from the fifth century.

Cranmer was only marginally involved in these struggles for influence; more seriously for his cause, the English people were not always as enthusiastic about change as he would have hoped. In 1549, a series of major disturbances broke out across England. As is always the case with such public disorder, the precise reasons for these uprisings were complex and varied, an opportunistic coalition of interests and grievances; but it was clear that resistance to the new Prayer Book and to its destruction of much of the medieval past was a prime cause for many. The regime had to work hard to subdue these acts of violence and sedition. Cranmer himself dramatically took to the pulpit of St Paul's Cathedral to issue a thundering rebuke to the leaders of the rebellion and call for a return to the unity and concord which he always took to be the sign of a country favoured with divine blessing. The government eventually had its way, but the episode had demonstrated the wisdom of its policy of a slow but purposeful process of reform.

Despite such pockets of resistance, if the Council had been allowed to continue to steer this course, England would have experienced a thorough Reformation which rivalled anything to be found in Zurich or Geneva. Cranmer's dream of making the country a model of reformed piety and its citizens shining examples of lives modelled in pure scriptural principles was within reach; so too was his ultimate goal of an international council on English soil and presided over by English prelates that bound together the Protestant world in belief and purpose. The young king might have gone down in history as the greatest champion of reformed belief and behaviour in Europe, the ruler under whose influence the Reformation found a whole nation in which to stand and to grow. Cranmer seems to have felt that he had further liturgical work to do in subsequent books of Common Prayer, and we can only speculate about how quickly he would also have severed England's ties to Catholic forms and structures of hierarchy, ceremony and clergy apparel, as many strong and senior voices were already encouraging him to do more intentionally.

It was not to be. The boy king developed tuberculosis early in 1553 and died, aged 15, on 6 July of that year. In increasing agony and despair, he and his Council tried to avert the religious disaster which they saw coming in the accession of Edward's half-sister Mary. Ultimately, though, the claims of a child of Henry VIII were always stronger than those of the obscure Lady Jane Grey, the King's reliably Protestant cousin, and the people's sympathies were with Mary, probably largely because of their perception of the injustice being done to her rather than real enthusiasm for her Catholicism. Cranmer was not a prominent figure in the attempt to subvert the succession, despite what must have been very severe anxieties about Mary's intentions. His efforts to persuade the King against the plan having failed, he duly signed the papers that would have placed Jane on the throne. Good intentions and scruples about this action were of no avail when Mary swept aside Northumberland's forces to assume the throne: and then punish her opponents. After a period of uncertainty and a tense hiatus of a few weeks, Cranmer was arrested and sent to the Tower after stubbornly – and bravely – refusing to back down on a public declaration against the resumption of the Mass.

Clearly, Cranmer knew his hour had come and was ready to face it. He encouraged others to flee and yet remained steadfastly himself at his post. There now began a very long and very gruelling series of incarcerations, interrogations, disputations and trials which lasted for two and a half years. The new regime hoped to force the Archbishop into a reversal and repudiation of his reforms and back into obedience to Rome, in order to make an example of the man who had, in Mary's eyes, been the source of the heresy by declaring her parents' marriage invalid and then its prime promulgator with the Edwardian reforms. The Queen was also clear about her intention to proceed, not by virtue of the royal supremacy but rather by restored papal authority in depriving and sentencing Cranmer. He had, after all, received his high office from the Pope's hand; Mary wanted him to lose it too in that manner, a public rebuke of his faithlessness. It was messy though, and Cranmer had to be legally relieved of the exercise of his office in the autumn of 1553, by virtue of the very royal supremacy which Mary so despised.

Already convicted of treason, Cranmer was sent, along with his colleagues and friends Bishops Hugh Latimer and Nicholas Ridley, to Oxford, for an examination of his alleged heresies. Here, the regime began by holding a series of disputations on the Eucharist, in which the three prelates acquitted themselves well. Their treatment in Oxford was reasonable: clearly, a long imprisonment was being envisaged as part of the intent of slowly wearing down these three chief protagonists. Matters came into sharper focus when England was finally reconciled to Rome and the papacy in November 1554, although Cardinal Reginald Pole did not formally succeed Cranmer as Archbishop until a year thereafter. Cranmer was tried by the Pope's command – this extra layer of bureaucracy accounts also for this lengthy delay – in September of 1555; he was combative and articulate and, apart from the public relations disaster of admitting that the Emperor Nero had indeed exercised royal supremacy, put up a strong show. The inevitable conviction followed, nevertheless. Ridley and Latimer were tried as second-tier prisoners slightly later and similarly condemned to die.

It is at this point, after two years of imprisonment and endless uncertainty about his fate, that Cranmer's last passion truly began in earnest. He was made to watch the burning of Ridley and Latimer from the roof of his prison on 16 October, before transfer to house arrest at Christ Church, where he was constantly under pressure from Catholic theologians sent to dispute with him. From now on, he was virtually alone, apart from the ministrations of a young Catholic attendant, Nicholas Woodson. With no other human companion, Cranmer seems to have repudiated parts of his earlier belief in order to maintain this poignant friendship. His first few offerings of such recantation, however, were withdrawn after consideration, and the prisoner was transferred back to jail. He endured the humiliating spectacle of a 'disgrading' ceremony, in which he was ceremonially stripped of his archbishop's robes, but did his utmost to disrupt the occasion, appealing to Rome and disputing the credentials of Bishop Edmund Bonner, his chief and merciless tormentor.[16] Even now harassed and pressed by his captors on central questions of belief, Cranmer remained defiant.

On 24 February 1556, the writ was issued for his burning, set for two weeks later. Physically weak, emotionally manipulated and psychologically tortured, utterly alone, facing a horrible death and deprived of all human comfort, Cranmer now experienced some sort of breakdown the sheer agony of which we can only imagine. In its midst, he signed a full recantation of his Protestant views and submitted to the Pope's authority. If he hoped thereby to win his life, he was again devastated by the news a few days later that Mary still considered death the only appropriate punishment for his crimes. Another, even more detailed repudiation of his own former views followed, including his writings on the Eucharist. But it was all useless. Tormented with guilt and confusion, visited by disturbing dreams, Cranmer prepared to die. At some point, however, perhaps even on the last full day of his life, his intentions shifted, and he determined to deny the regime its triumph.

Cranmer's last moments are the stuff of Protestant legend, thanks to the work of John Foxe, whose full account of them is contained later in this book. Led in the rain to St Mary's Church, the condemned man sat through an excoriating sermon by Dr Henry Cole, clearly and naturally in a state of heightened emotion. When asked to deliver his final words, intended to be a last contrite statement of his error and his responsibility

---

16 For Foxe's full account of Cranmer's disgrading, see Chapter 6.

for leading the realm into schism and heresy, Cranmer dramatically announced that he did indeed regret some of his views and writings: specifically, the recantations he had recently signed. As the audience began to recognize the import of this unexpected shift in the content of his speech, Cranmer got into his stride, denouncing the Pope's 'false doctrine' and reaffirming that the *Defence* and *Answer* represented his mature and final eucharistic theology. He would die a Protestant, and the hand that had signed away the great achievements of his life and the fruit of his evangelical convictions at a stroke would be the first to burn. Led to the stake, amid scenes of extraordinary chaos and commotion, he did indeed hold his right hand in the flame until it was charred, before himself submitting to the fire and smoke.

It may be that the emphasis given to these last, dramatic and heroic moments in the collective memory has sometimes overshadowed the real achievements of Thomas Cranmer's life. He held the highest office in the Church in England for twenty years, one constant force amid rapid change and turbulent political circumstances. As the Christian world convulsed and fragmented, riven by bitter discord and violent disagreement, he crafted in England a new and stable settlement, thoroughly reformed and adorned with an incomparable liturgical expression. He brought to the theological undergirding of this English Church a depth and breadth of scholarly acumen hardly rivalled by any of his successors, while never losing his commitment to and compassion for the English people, nor his sense that their spiritual needs were his prime responsibility. In private life and public affairs, Cranmer was courageous when required and, for the most part, compromising only when he judged it wise in the ultimate furtherance of his goals. His complicity in some matters, especially the monstrous treatment of Catherine of Aragon, certainly repels us and may cause many to judge his connivance harshly. Such judgements, however, are always made from the easy vantage point of those entirely remote from the circumstances. Cranmer at other times and places was a strong and forceful advocate for those accused, friendless and alone; and he endured his own downfall with principled dignity and resolute courage, once Mary's accession was assured.

John Knox, the chief architect of the Scottish Reformation, and a fierce and savage critic of those who stood in his way, including Cranmer during a fight over the 1552 Prayer Book, once referred to the Archbishop as 'the mild man of God'.[17] He may not wholeheartedly

---

17 MacCulloch, *Thomas Cranmer*, p. 622.

have intended it as a compliment, but it reflects the consistent verdict of those who dealt with Cranmer in person. Though passionate in his cause and utterly devoted to his interpretation of Christian religion, Cranmer remained merciful, compassionate and courteous: except perhaps where Stephen Gardiner was concerned, but there he had regularly suffered immense provocation. Glimpses of this humanity can be seen at every turn in his life: seeking to mitigate Thomas More's dire situation and honour his friendship with the King by sparing his life, spending the night offering comfort and companionship to the distraught but immensely foolish Catherine Howard, forgiving his political enemies after numerous attempts to remove him, caring for the welfare of servants and tenants, honouring promises of financial aid made by his predecessors and seeking the safety of other evangelicals endangered by Mary's rule without bothering for his own. It may not be too fanciful, indeed, to suggest that the godfather of the Anglican spiritual tradition invested it with something of his own character: generosity, compassion and a breadth of heart and vision. It is to be hoped that the global Communion which is in many ways the child of his religious genius can live up to such virtues in the years ahead of it.

The King's Great Matter: Cranmer and Henry VIII

The Royal Supremacy

During the late 1520s and early 1530s, England was convulsed by the King's 'Great Matter': his desire to divorce his queen, Catherine of Aragon, and his quest for papal dispensation to allow him to do so. Henry grew convinced that the lack of a male heir indicated divine disapproval of the arrangement, blessed by the Pope, by which he had married the widow of his elder brother, Prince Arthur, in 1509. He also grew increasingly enamored of the Lady Anne Boleyn, one of Catherine's ladies at court, who in turn shrewdly resisted all his efforts to make her his mistress, insisting on a marriage. These two great passions drove the King towards separation from Rome, and the eventual triggering of religious change in England through the sixteenth century. In the end, the annulment of the King's marriage was possible only through taking matters into his own hands and declaring the fact of his 'royal supremacy': that, as King, he held absolute authority, not only over the lands and loyalties of England and the English but also over their spiritual lives, and therefore over the English Church. The papal supremacy, Henry's theologians declared, was a monstrous and yet hitherto unrealized and unchallenged attack on the rights and prerogatives of English kings. It had been a usurpation of authority that did not belong to Rome, and an outrageous occupation by stealth of a significant portion of royal sway. Henry, increasingly desperate to have his way over the marriage, was understandably delighted with this discovery; and the Royal Supremacy was slowly implemented in the early 1530s through a series of bold legislative measures.

The Royal Supremacy was an idea with obvious attractiveness to most English people, who have always enjoyed an opportunity to prove themselves superior to continental Europeans and their exotic habits. Only those who cherished England's ancient ties of religious identity and uniformity with the rest of Christendom upheld the papal authority over the English Church. It was all too easy for the King to marginalize these die-hards as traitors; and thus Bishop John Fisher and Sir Thomas More eventually suffered death for their convictions. That said, the supremacy was a new idea (or at least an old one rediscovered), and had to be carefully inculcated into the hearts and minds of the people. Thomas Cranmer came to the dizzying heights of the archiepiscopal throne quite unused to and unprepared for the daunting national task before him, of tidying up the King's nearly ten-year quest for a divorce and rooting the basis for the divorce and the breach with Rome it entailed deeply in the English consciousness. He brought to both tasks, so vital in the shaping of all subsequent English Christianity, a zeal and determination which won him the King's undying favour and gratitude ever after, a favour, indeed, which protected him through very dark days in which many of his closest colleagues perished.

We begin with documents which illustrate Cranmer's convictions about the supremacy, and his actions to enforce it and enact the King's divorce. The first is a letter of June 1533 to his friend and confidant, Nicholas Hawkins, the Archdeacon of Ely and one of the King's ambassadors in Europe, describing the proceedings in Dunstable which pronounced the first marriage void, and the coronation of Anne Boleyn which then followed.[1] The letter is a fascinating document, chronicling the end of papal authority in England, and the lavish ceremonial which accompanied Anne Boleyn's coronation, an event still couched in traditional forms but soon to lead to radical religious innovation. Cranmer goes on to speak of the case of John Frith, a man at this point condemned for holding a view of the Eucharist which in later years was to be Cranmer's own, and that of England's official liturgy. The paragraph illustrates England's share, both in the Reformation's division and its savage remedies for doctrinal difference.

As touching the final determination and concluding of the matter of divorce between my Lady Catherine and the King's Grace, which said matter, after the Convocation in that behalf had determined and agreed according to the former consent of the Universities, it was thought convenient by the King and his learned counsel, that I should repair unto Dunstable, which is within four miles unto Ampthill,

---

1 Cranmer held the divorce determination at Dunstable in May 1533 in order to be close to Queen Catherine, who was staying at Ampthill. Probably to Cranmer's relief, she refused to appear and made his task all the easier. Henry and Anne had been secretly married (not by Cranmer) in January.

where the Lady Catherine keepeth her house, and there to call her before me to hear the final sentence in the said matter. Notwithstanding, she would not at all obey thereunto, for when she was . . . cited to appear by a day, she utterly refused the same, saying, that inasmuch as her cause was before the Pope, she would have none other judge; and therefore would not take me for her judge . . . and the morrow after Ascension Day I gave final sentence therein, how that it was indispensible for the Pope to license any such marriages.

This done, and after our rejourneying home again, the King's Highness prepared all things convenient for the Coronation of the Queen, which was also after such a manner as followeth . . .

In the morning there assembled with me at Westminster Church, the Bishop of York, the Bishop of London, the Bishop of Winchester, the Bishop of Lincoln, the Bishop of Bath, and the Bishop of St. Asaph, the Abbot of Westminster, with ten or twelve more Abbots, which all revestred ourselves in our pontificalibus, and so furnished, with our crosses and croziers, proceeded out of the Abbey in a procession unto Westminster Hall, where we received the Queen apparelled in a robe of purple velvet, and all the ladies and gentlewomen in robes and gowns of scarlet, according to the manner used before time in such business: and so her Grace sustained of each side with two Bishops, the Bishop of London and the Bishop of Winchester, came forth in procession unto the Church of Westminster, she in her hair, my Lord of Suffolk bearing before her the Crown, and two other lords bearing also before her a Sceptre and a white rod, and so entered up into the high altar, where divers ceremonies used about her, I did set the Crown on her head, and then sing Te Deum, etc. And after that was sung a solemn mass, all which while her Grace sat crowned upon a scaffold, which was made between the high altar and the choir in Westminster Church; which mass and ceremonies done and finished, all the assembly of noblemen brought her into Westminster Hall again, where was kept a great solemn feast all day . . .

Other news have we none notable, but that one Frith, which was in the Tower in prison, was appointed by the King's Grace to be examined before me, my Lord of London, my Lord of Winchester, my Lord of Suffolk, my Lord Chancellor and my Lord of Wiltshire, whose opinion was so notably erroneous, that we could not dispatch him, was fain to leave him to the determination of his Ordinary, which is the Bishop of London. His said opinion is of such nature, that he thought it not necessary to be believed as an article of our faith, that there is the very corporeal presence of Christ within the host and sacrament of the altar, and holdeth after this point most after the opinion of Oecolampadius.[2] And surely I myself sent for him three or four times to persuade him to leave that his imagination, but for all that we could do therein, he would not apply to any counsel; notwithstanding now he is at a final end with all examinations, for my Lord of London hath given sentence and delivered him to the secular power, where he looketh every day to go unto the fire.[3]

In a second letter, Cranmer outlines to the King a sermon he has preached on the supremacy. It reveals the main contours of his argument and the intellectual and theological foundation on which Cranmer's understanding rested. It also shows, in a rare glimpse into Cranmer as preacher, the pains he took to disseminate the teaching of the King's spiritual authority carefully and yet committedly. In the preaching of the supremacy, however, Cranmer takes pains to introduce some themes of the Lutheran reformation against the papacy, especially concerning the tension between faith and works. The letter is probably datable to 1536, a year in which the Archbishop preached widely on the subject, including at the national pulpit at St Paul's Cross.[4]

Pleaseth it your Grace to be advertised, that where as well by your Grace's special letters . . . as also by mouth in Winchester at Michaelmas last past, your Grace commanded all the prelates of your realm, that they with all acceleration and expedition should do their diligence every one in his diocese, fully to persuade your people of the Bishop of Rome his authority, that it is but a false and unjust usurpation, and that your Grace, of very right and by God's law, is the supreme head of this Church of England, next immediately unto God; I, to accomplish your Grace's commandment . . . came up into these parts of East Kent, only by preaching to persuade the people in the said two articles: and in mine own church at Canterbury, because I was informed that that town in those two points was least persuaded of all my diocese, I preached there two sermons myself . . .

---

2 A German reformer, 1482–1531, early champion of the theology of Martin Luther and then priest and scholar in Basel, where he enjoyed also the friendship and patronage of Zwingli.

3 Thomas Cranmer, *The Remains of Thomas Cranmer*, ed. Henry Jenkyns, 4 vols (Oxford: Oxford University Press, 1833), vol. 1, pp. 27–32.

4 As later recorded by the Catholic polemicist Nicholas Harpsfield in his very biased but fascinating account of the 'pretended divorce' of Henry and Catherine; see, for instance, J. Ridley, *Thomas Cranmer* (Oxford: Clarendon Press, 1962), p. 98.

The scope and effect of both my sermons stood in three things. First, I declared that the Bishop of Rome was not God's vicar in earth, as he was taken. And although it is so taught these three or four hundred years, yet it is done by means of the Bishop of Rome, who compelled men by oaths so to teach, to the maintenance of his authority, contrary to God's word. And here I declared by what means and craft the Bishops of Rome obtained and usurped authority.

Second, because the see of Rome was called 'Sancta Sedes Romana' and the Bishop was called 'Sanctissimus Papa',[5] and men's consciences peradventure could not be quiet to be separated from so holy a place, and from God's most holy vicar; I showed the people, that this thing ought nothing to move them, for it was but a holiness in name . . .

Third, I spake against the Bishop of Rome his laws; which he calleth 'Divinas Leges' and 'Sacros Canones',[6] and makes them equal with God's law. And here I declared that many of the laws were very contrary; and some of them which were good and laudable, yet they were not of such holiness as he would make them; that is, to be taken as God's laws, or to have remission of sins by observing them. And here I said, that so many of his laws as were good, men ought not to contemn[7] or despise them, and willfully to break them; for those that be good your Grace had received as laws of your realm, until such time as others should be made. And therefore as laws of your realm they must be observed, and not contemned.

And here I spake as well of the ceremonies of the Church as of the foresaid laws; that they ought neither to be rejected or despised, nor yet to be observed with this opinion, that they of themselves make men holy, or that they remit sins. For seeing that our sins be remitted by the death of our Saviour Christ Jesus, I said it was too much injury to Christ, to impute the remission of our sins to any laws or ceremonies of man's making. Nor the laws and ceremonies of the Church at their first making were ordained for that intent. But as the common laws of your Grace's realm be not made to remit sins, nor no man doth observe them for that intent, but for a common commodity, and for a good order and quietness to be observed among your subjects; even so were the laws and ceremonies first instituted in the Church for a good order, and for remembrances of many good things, but not for remission of our sins. And though it be good to observe them

---

5 'The Holy seat of Rome'; 'Most Holy Father'.
6 'Sacred laws'; 'divinely ordained rules'.
7 'hold them in contempt'.

well for that intent they were first ordained; yet it is not good, but a contumely unto Christ, to observe them with this opinion, that they remit sins; or that the very bare observation of them in itself is a holiness before God: although they be remembrances of many holy things, or a disposition unto goodness. And even so do the laws of your Grace's realm dispose men unto justice, unto peace, and other true and perfect holiness. Wherefore I did conclude for a general rule, that the people ought to observe them, as they do the laws of your Grace's realm, and with no more opinion of holiness, or remission of sin, than the other common laws of your Grace's realm.[8]

The Institution of a Christian Man

The same year, 1536, saw the publication of Ten Articles, the first doctrinal statement of the Church of England. The articles were prefaced by a statement in the King's name, assuming rather than explaining his supremacy in spiritual matters, and were rather traditional in character, affirming transubstantiation and the validity of some forms of ceremonial and imagery in devotion. A year later, in 1537, the English bishops produced a book in committee intended further to instil the idea and fact of the supremacy into English minds, and offer a more detailed statement of essential Christian belief as the English now understood it. Titled *The Institution of a Christian Man*, it outlined and expanded on the creed, the sacraments, still seven in number, the Ten Commandments and the Lord's Prayer and *Ave Maria*. Given the collaborative nature of the book, and the constant difficulty of knowing the mind of the King, the result often seems cautious in its theological explanations despite efforts by Cranmer to push it in a more reforming direction,[9] as with the defence of preaching outlined below. One matter, however, is very clear: the royal supremacy is firmly defended as divine law, and its effects and advantages are glowingly described.

Within this realm the presentation and nomination of the bishoprics appertaineth unto the kings of this realm, and of other lesser cures and personages some unto the king's highness, some unto other noble men, some unto bishops and some unto other persons, whom we call the patrons of the benefices . . . and unto the priests and bishops

---

8 Cranmer, *Remains*, Vol. I, pp. 167–9.

9 For more on this, see Eamon Duffy, *The Stripping of the Altars* (New Haven and London: Yale University Press, 1992), p. 401.

belongeth by the authority of the gospel to approve and confirm the person, which shall be by the king's highness or the other patrons so nominated, elected and presented unto them to have the cure of these certain people, within the certain parish or diocese, or else to reject him, as was said before, from the same, for his demerits or unworthiness. For surely the office of preaching is the chief and most principal office, whereunto priests or bishops be called by the authority of the gospel, and they be also called bishops and archbishops, that is to say superattendants or overseers specially to signify that is their office to oversee, to watch and to look diligently upon their flock, and to cause that Christ's doctrine and his religion may be truly and sincerely conserved, taught and set forth among Christian people.

. . . Moreover, the truth is, that God constituted and ordained the authority of Christian kings and princes to be the most high and supreme above all other powers and offices in the regiment and governance of his people: and committed unto them, as unto the chief heads of their commonwealths, the cure and oversight of all the people, which be within their realms and dominions, without any exception. And unto them of right and by God's commandment belongeth, not only to prohibit unlawful violence, to correct offenders . . . to conserve moral honesty among their subjects according to the laws of their realm, to defend Justice, and to procure the public weal, and the common peace and tranquillity in outward and earthly things: but specially and principally to defend the faith of Christ and his religion, to conserve and maintain the true doctrine of Christ, and all such as be true preachers and setters forth thereof, and to abolish all abuses, heresies and idolatries, which be brought in . . .

And therefore whereas the king's most royal majesty, considering of his most excellent wisdom, not only the notable decay of Christ's true and perfect religion amongst us, but also the intolerable thraldom, captivity and bondage, with the infinite damages and prejudices, which we and other his subjects continually sustained, by reason of that long usurped and abused power, which the Bishops of Rome were wont to exercise here in this realm, hath now of his most godly disposition . . . determined no longer to suffer the Bishop of Rome to execute any part of his jurisdiction here within this realm, but clearly to deliver us from the same, and restore us again to our old liberty.[10]

---

10 *The Institution of a Christian Man* (London, 1537), fols 43v–44r, 49v–50v.

There are glimpses in the *Institution*, perhaps, of more poetic Cranmerian touches and flourishes. The extended interpretation of the Lord's Prayer perhaps works as well as anything in the book, which otherwise tends necessarily to an excessive emphasis on orthodoxy and the burden of inculcating it placed on local priests. Here, as an example of the more beautiful elements of the book, is the elaboration of the phrase, 'give us this day our daily bread', offering a sensitive picture of the bonds of charity and community by which sixteenth-century English society was held together:

Our heavenly Father, we beseech thee, give us this day our daily bread. Give us meat, drink, and clothing for our bodies. Send us increase of corn, fruit and cattle. Give us health and strength, rest and peace, that we may lead a peacable and quiet life in all godliness and honesty. Grant us good success in all our business, and help in adversity and peril. Grant us, we beseech thee, all things convenient for our necessity in this temporal life. And to them, to whom thou dost vouchsafe to give more than their own portion necessary for their vocation, and degree: give thy grace, that they may be thy diligent and true dispensators and stewards, to distribute that they have (over and above that is necessary, considering their estate and degree) to them that have need of it. For lo, good Lord, thou dost provide for thy poor people, that have nothing: by them which have of thy gift sufficient to relieve them self and other. And give also thy grace to us, that we have not too much solicitude and care for these transitory and unstable things: but that our hearts may be fixed in things, which be eternal, and in thy kingdom, which is everlasting. And yet moreover, good Lord, not only give us our necessaries: but also conserve that, thou dost give us, and cause that it may come to our use, and by us to the poor people, for whom by us thou hast provided. Give us grace, that we may be fed and nourished with all the life of Christ, that is to say, both his words and works.[11]

In one major theological area of the Reformation debates, the *Institution* tried to chart a more evangelical course than the English Church hitherto had embraced. Cranmer's enthusiasm for Luther's famous and central claim, that humanity is put into right relationship with God only by faith in Christ and not by any works or deeds which might precede or accompany it, was fairly clear, but brought him into conflict

---

11 *Institution*, fol. 81r–v.

with the King's more traditional conservatism and orthodox Catholicism. The *Institution*, almost as an afterthought it seems, includes an 'Article of Justification', which tries at least to place faith as the 'horse' which draws the 'cart' of Christian works and charity which must follow it. It then goes on to emphasize the believer's inner spiritual growth and to undermine any confidence in the mere mechanistic performance of charitable deeds as a guarantor of divine regard. It represented a critical passage in support of Cranmer's claim that the *Bishops' Book* was a reforming document.

> As touching the order and cause of our justification, we think it convenient, that all bishops and preachers shall instruct and teach the people, committed unto their spiritual charge, that this word, Justification, signifieth remission of our sins, and our acceptation or reconciliation into the grace and favour of God, that is to say, our perfect renovation in Christ.
>
> ITEM, that sinners attain this justification by contrition and faith joined with charity, after such sort and manner as is before mentioned and declared in the sacrament of penance. Not as though our contrition or faith, or any works proceeding thereof, can worthily merit or deserve to attain the said justification. For the only mercy and grace of the Father, promised freely unto us for his son's sake Jesus Christ, and the merits of his blood and passion, be the only sufficient and worthy causes thereof. And yet that notwithstanding to the attaining of the same justification, God requireth to be in us, not only inward contrition, perfect faith, and charity, certain hope and confidence, with all other spiritual graces and motions, which as was said before, must necessarily concur in remission of our sins, that is to say, our justification: but also he requireth and commandeth us, that after we be justified, we must also have good works of charity and obedience towards God, in the observing and fulfilling outwardly of his laws and commandments. For though acceptation and everlasting life be conjoined with justification: yet our good works be necessarily required to the attaining of everlasting life . . . wherefore all good Christian people must understand and believe certainly, that God necessarily requireth of us to do good works commanded by him, and that not only outward and civil works, but also the inward spiritual motions and grace of the Holy Ghost, that is to say, to dread and fear God, to love God, to have firm confidence and trust in God, to invocate and call upon God, to have patience in all adversities, to hate sin and to have certain purpose and will not to sin

again, and such other like motions and virtues. For Christ saith, we must not only do outward civil good works, but we must also have these foresaid inward spiritual motions, consenting and agreeable to the law of God.[12]

We cannot be sure that these words are entirely Cranmer's but, as the chair of the committee that produced them, his role must have been key. A further indication of his commitment to the book, and especially to this emphasis on faith as the main factor in justification, exists in the correspondence he entered upon with the King about it. Fascinatingly, a copy of the *Institution* survives complete with the King's annotations. They are varied in character, but of particular interest are the King's various suggestions that the book needed to emphasize the place of human effort in acquiring a right relationship with God rather more forcefully. Cranmer's responses to these suggestions also survive, and reveal his willingness to take the King on, quite sharply on occasion, when he felt that truth was at stake. The exchange lays bare the division between Henry's traditional emphasis on the need for 'works' in the Christian life and the Archbishop's desire to promote the role of faith, in a more thoroughgoing, Lutheran vein. Arguably, it also points to a general character trait in the King, an insistence on an absolute following of the rules and a merciless attitude towards those who fail to observe them. Henry was to use such a punitive attitude ferociously against advisors, friends and even wives on numerous occasions when they disappointed him or seemed to lack in loyalty. Cranmer deftly critiques such an understanding, emphasizing rather the mercy of God and the inherent good works which are always the fruit of a proper faith. In the following extract, Cranmer is responding to Henry's annotation to a sentence on the believer's status as God's 'servant and his own son by adoption and grace and the right inheritor of his kingdom', in which he desires the caveat to be inserted: 'as long as I persevere in his precepts and laws'. The Archbishop is having none of it, nor of the weakening of the language it would entail.

What love so ever the son pretendeth unto his father, or the servant unto his master, yet surely all that love is but coloured and feigned, if they be not glad to accomplish the will and commandments of their father and master, and very loath and sorry to transgress any part thereof. Likewise, how can the son persuade with himself that his

---

12 *Institution*, fol. 96r–v.

father loveth him, favoureth him, and will do all good for him, and at length make him his heir, if he love not his father, nor be sorry to offend his father, but, like an unnatural and disobedient child, is ready to follow his own sensual mind, and to rebel against his father and all his precepts? It is not possible that such a son should have a sure trust of his father's benignity, gracious goodness, and fatherly love towards him, unless it come either of the ignorance or else the iniquity of his father; so that he either dissemble with his father, and trust that his father knoweth not of his folly, disobedience and rebellion; or else that he know that his father be so evil himself, that he favoureth ill-doers, and delighteth in the iniquity of his son, and loveth him never the worse for his vicious living. But to God (who knoweth all things, even before they be done, and knoweth all men's hearts even to the bottom better than they do themselves, and who also can favour no iniquity or malice of sin, but hateth it and the doers of the same,) cannot be ascribed any ignorance or evilness. Therefore, let no man deceive his own mind; for no man surely can have the right faith and sure trust of God's favour towards him, and persuade with himself that God is his benign and loving Father, and taketh him for his well-beloved son and heir, except he love God in his heart, and have a willing and glad mind, and a delight to do all things that may please God, and a very great repentance and sorrow that ever he did anything that did offend and displease so loving a Father, whose goodness he can never account.[13]

Elsewhere, Henry's attempted interpolations of phrases such as 'and do our duty' and 'as long as we live as we ought' are similarly and increasingly urgently resisted. Though the King's suggestions largely failed to make the final copy, the *Institution* itself did not gain the royal approval Cranmer and Cromwell sought, and thus became colloquially known as *The Bishops' Book*. The *Necessary Doctrine and Erudition for Any Christian Man*, published in 1543, did carry the King's offical authority, but represented a defeat for Cranmer and the reforming party in pushing English Christianity back to a more traditional religious expression. Its familiar title – *The King's Book* – reflected the Archbishop's lack of involvement in its compilation. Its own article on justification revealed the renewed theological conservatism of the

---

13 Thomas Cranner, *The works of Thomas Cranmer, Archbishop of Canterbury, Martyr 1556*, 2 vols, ed. John Edmund Cox (Cambridge: Parker Society, 1884–6), vol. 2, *Miscellaneous writings and letters*, pp. 84–6, 110.

1540s, mentioning faith only in passing and stressing much more the system of obligatory sacramental and charitable activity with which medieval Catholics had been more familiar. It also added another article on good works, for good measure. Cranmer was having to bide his time amid choppier ecclesiastical waters.

Cranmer as Bishop and Pastor

Thomas Cranmer came to the throne of Canterbury having served only the living of Bredon in Worcestershire as priest, for two years prior to the whirlwind promotion. The rectory of Bredon had been a sign of favour, stemming from his exertions to secure the divorce in Europe and, given the extent of his diplomatic career and travels on the King's behalf overseas, it is doubtful that Cranmer spent much time in Bredon or attempting the cure of souls. Once he was installed and enthroned as Archbishop, Cranmer found himself with a new range of unfamiliar responsibilities. He was in charge of a large and diverse diocese, in which official religious policy needed to be inculcated and enforced. He was the spiritual leader of the Province of Canterbury too; and he soon found himself embroiled in turf battles with other more conservative bishops about his visitation rights in their dioceses, as the full implications of the royal supremacy were worked out, and his role and title of 'Metropolitan', carried by all his successors to the present day, was defined. Finally, Cranmer after his elevation was chief chaplain to the royal family itself. In this role, he has attracted both scorn and admiration: scorn from those who have seen in the remaining records of his dealings with monarchs only subservience and a spineless acceptance of royal command; and admiration from those who see beneath the surface deference a more steely core.

What is beyond dispute is that King Henry VIII always felt the deepest fondness for his Archbishop.[14] Cranmer was always to enjoy a special and secure place in Henry's affections, when he handed the King what Henry had so desired for so long, after years of wasted disputes, dashed hopes, fruitless diplomatic missions and – let us speak clearly – frustrated lust for Anne Boleyn. It seems that others at court recognized this too, and saw in Cranmer a man who could be the bearer of bad news, as when, in 1541, he was deputed to inform the King of

---

14 See above, p. 9, for Ralph Morice's account of Thomas Cromwell's sense of this affection.

the serial infidelities of Queen Catherine Howard, a task he performed
without any pleasure or relish but with a heart whose heaviness we can only
imagine. Before that, he had written a famous letter to the King concerning
the entirely false and fabricated charges of infidelity levelled against Anne
Boleyn by Thomas Cromwell and those now ranged against her in the
royal household. As Diarmaid MacCulloch has pointed out, it is a letter
whose defence of Queen Anne is rather striking, despite the courteous and
careful language which has caused some to see it as craven and cowardly.[15]
He wrote a rather similar letter, equally gentle and yet equally firm, in
defence of the very man whose subterfuge had brought the Queen down,
Thomas Cromwell, when he faced his own fall from grace in 1540. Both
letters, read aright, reveal him as a man prepared to be the last friend to
one entirely abandoned by the King and those closest to him, and therefore
a man of greater courage than some have allowed. Even the universally rejected Catherine Howard, guilty of reckless, foolish, almost suicidal crimes
after her debauches, found in the Archbishop a final confessor and personal chaplain whose gentleness and pastoral skill were perhaps her only
comfort in her final days of absolute breakdown.

As illustration of these duties and tasks, a selection of excerpts from
Cranmer's letters is offered in two groups. First, a few which show
Cranmer at work as bishop: guiding priests and parishes, making peace
within and between them and offering insight and wisdom, both in
the Canterbury Diocese and at court, in a range of ways. His predomi-
nant concerns seem consistent throughout: the need for conscientious,
resident and committed priests, who take trouble to offer guidance and
godly education to their parishioners; unity and concord among communities and within churches; and adherence to the King's authority
and to the Church in England, unsullied by residual allegiance to Rome
or to the Pope. After these are some rather personal letters, often printed
elsewhere, which demonstrate the Archbishop acting as chaplain to
royalty in the skilful, devoted manner described.

Letter to Master Stapleton, Parson of Byngham (12 October 1533)

In my right hearty wise I commend me unto you: signifying to the
same, that I am right glad to hear such good report of you as I do,
as well in that ye be so effectuously minded and given to see your
pastoral cure discharged by your continual preaching and teaching,

---

15 Diarmaid MacCulloch, *Thomas Cranmer* (New Haven and London: Yale
University Press, 1996), pp. 156–9.

as also in confirming the same by your good conversation, example of living, and charitable behaviour towards your neighbours, whereunto I exhort you in Christ's behalf to go forward and proceed, as ye have hitherto right well begun. And where also I am advertized, that by your both good provision, and provident wisdom, there is a free school maintained with you for the virtuous bringing up of youth, I heartily require you, inasmuch as with this bearer I send now unto you my sister's son, named Thomas Rosell, apt (as I suppose) to learning, that ye will at this my attemptation and request, do so much as to see him ordered and instruct in such doctrine as shall be convenient both for his age and capacity. And for those your pains in so doing, I will always be ready to show unto you like pleasure. Thus fare you well.

Letter to my Wellbeloved the Inhabitants of Hadleigh (20 March 1534)[16]

In my right hearty wise I commend me unto you. And sorry I am to hear there is lack of charity, and also be many grudges amongst you, you all being Christian men which should be of such charity and unity as if ye were but one body. And to the intent that ye should be so, and that ye should the rather be induced to concord, and specially against this good time, I have desired the bearer, Master Hugh Vaughan, to take the pain to come unto you now with these my letters, and to exhort you all in my name and on my behalf, and most specially in the name of our Lord, that you and every one of you put away such grudges as ye have one against another, and become lovers together as children of God ought to do: (for whosoever is out of charity, do what he will, it is not acceptable in the sight of God: and how can he love God that hateth his Christian brother, which is the creature of God) so to continue in charity here in this world together as the sons of one Father, our Lord in heaven, that ye may be beloved of him after in heaven.

---

16 Hadleigh in Suffolk had a turbulent existence through the English Reformations. Cranmer in this letter is arguing in favour of a known evangelical, Thomas Rose, who enjoyed the Archbishop's strong patronage. It is a window into Cranmer's episcopal life, showing not only his support for reforming priests but also his insistence on parochial unity; see MacCulloch, *Thomas Cranmer*, p. 110.

[Cranmer rehearses the charges against the Curate, about one of his sermons, and continues] . . . I have sent the said Curate to you again, desiring you which have not been his friends heretofore to leave your grudges, and you all to accept him favourably, the rather for this my writing. Not intending hereby, but if you or any of you shall have just cause against him hereafter, you shall and may prosecute the same according to justice; for it is not mine intent in any wise hereby to let[17] justice, if it be justly prosecuted, without great and probable suspicion of malice and calumnious accusation. And if any of you shall have at any time hereafter and just cause to sue afore me, ye shall be sure of such favour as I may lawfully show unto you.

Letter to Hugh Latimer (Early in 1534)

Hugh Latimer, later Bishop of Worcester and famously martyred under Queen Mary, was in 1534 a priest famed for his eloquent espousal of the evangelical cause, for which he had sometimes attracted controversy, as this letter reflects. Cranmer used his patronage to appoint him the Lenten preacher at Court; this letter intriguingly displays the care Cranmer took to ensure that this was not a disastrous failure for the cause, so dear to him, of shaping Christianity in England away from Roman Catholic belief and practice. He warns Latimer about the caution needed concerning subject matter, causing controversy, and overtaxing the King's limited, though still impressive, attention span.

I commend me unto you, etc. There be to certify you of the King's pleasure, how that his Grace is contented that ye shall be admitted to preach on all the Wednesdays of this next Lent before him. Whereupon I thought it very expedient, for divers considerations reasonably me moving thereto, to admonish you of certain things in no wise to be neglect and omitted on your behalf, in time of your preaching; which to observe and follow according to mine advice hereafter to you prescribed, shall at the length redound to your no little laud and praise.

First, therefore, take this order, (if ye will) reading over the book ye take for your purpose some processes of Scripture, the Gospel, Epistle, or any other part of Scripture in the Bible, and the same to expound and declare according to the pure sense and meaning thereof; wherein, above all things it will be most convenient, that ye do not at all persuade for the defence of your own causes and matters

---

17 'hinder'.

lately in controversy; but that ye rather do seem utterly [to pass over] those your accusations, than now in that place any sparkle of suspicion of grudge should appear to remain in you for the same. This done, that likewise ye be very circumspect to overpass and omit all manner speech, either apertly or suspiciously sounding against any special man's facts, acts, manners or sayings, to the intent your audience have none occasion thereby, namely to slander your adversaries; which would seem to many that you were void of charity, and so much the more unworthy to occupy that room. Nevertheless, if such occasion be given by the word of God, let none offence or superstition be unreprehended, specially if it be generally spoken, without affection.

Furthermore, I would ye should so study to comprehend your matters, that in any condition you stand no longer in the pulpit than an hour, or an hour and a half at the most, for by long expense of time the King and the Queen shall peradventure wax so weary at the beginning, that they shall have small delight to continue throughout with you to the end. Therefore let the effect of the premises take no place in your mind, specially before this circumspect audience, to the intent that you in so doing need not to have any other declaration hereafter against the misreports of your adversaries. And for your further instruction in this behalf, I would ye should the sooner come up to London, here to prepare all things in a readiness, according to such expectation as is had in you.

Letter to King Henry VIII (3 May 1536)

Perhaps the most famous of Cranmer's letters, and unjustly criticized in the past, this heartfelt plea for Anne Boleyn's case to be carefully weighed and considered, along with a firm statement of Cranmer's faith in her, reveals gentle courage, pastoral sensitivity to the emotional pain involved and a commitment to justice in this most dramatic situation, whose consequences he well knew could have profound implications for the nation and the Church.

Pleaseth it your most noble Grace to be advertised, that at your Grace's commandment by Mr. Secretary's letters, written in your Grace's name, I came to Lambeth yesterday, and do there remain to know your Grace's farther pleasure. And forsomuch as, without your Grace's commandment, I dare not, contrary to the contents of the said letters, presume to come unto your Grace's presence; nevertheless, of my most bounden duty, I can do no less than most humbly to desire your Grace, by your great wisdom, and by the assistance of God's help, somewhat to suppress the deep sorrow of your Grace's heart, and to take all adversities of God's hand both patiently and thankfully. I cannot deny but your Grace hath great causes many ways of lamentable heaviness: and also that, in the wrongful estimation of the world, your Grace's honour of every part is highly touched (whether the things that commonly be spoken of be true or not), that I remember not that ever Almighty God sent unto your Grace any like occasion to try your Grace's constancy throughout, whether your Highness can be content to take of God's hand, as well things displeasant as pleasant. And if he find in your most noble heart such an obedience unto his will, that your Grace without murmuration and overmuch heaviness, do accept all adversities, not less thanking him than when all things succeed after your Grace's will and pleasure, nor less procuring his glory and honour; then I suppose your Grace did never thing more acceptable unto him, since your first governance of this your realm. And moreover, your Grace shall give unto him occasion to multiply and increase his graces and benefits unto your highness, as he did unto his most faithful servant Job; unto whom, after his great calamities and heaviness, for his obedient heart, and willing acceptation of God's scourge and rod, 'addidit ei Dominus cuncta duplicia'.[18] And if it be true, that is openly reported of the Queen's Grace, if men had a right estimation of things, they should not esteem any part of your Grace's honour to be touched thereby, but her honour only to be clearly disparaged. And I am in such a perplexity, that my mind is clean amazed: for I never had better opinion in woman than I had in her; which maketh me to think that she should not be culpable. And again, I think your highness would not have gone so far, except she had surely been culpable. Now I think that your Grace best knoweth, that, next unto your Grace, I was most bound unto her of all creatures living. Wherefore, I most humbly beseech your Grace, to suffer me in that, which both God's law, nature, and also her kindness bindeth me unto; that is, that I may with your Grace's favour, wish and pray for her, that she may declare herself inculpable and innocent. And if she be found culpable, considering your Grace's goodness towards her, and from what condition your Grace of your only mere goodness took her, and set the crown upon her head; I repute him not

---

18 'God gave to him twice as much as he had before' (Job 42.10).

your Grace's faithful servant and subject, nor true unto the realm, that would not desire the offence without mercy to be punished, to the example of all other. And as I loved her not a little, for the love which I judged her to bear towards God and his Gospel; so, if she be proved culpable, there is not one that loveth God and his gospel that ever will favour her, but must hate her above all other; and the more they favour the Gospel, the more they will hate her: for then there was never creature in our time that so much slandered the Gospel. And God hath sent her this punishment, for that she feignedly hath professed his Gospel in her mouth, and not in heart and deed. And though she have offended so, that she hath deserved never to be reconciled unto your Grace's favour; yet Almighty God hath manifoldly declared his goodness towards your Grace, and never offended you. But your Grace, I am sure, acknowledgeth that you have offended him. Wherefore, I trust that your Grace will bear no less entire favour unto the truth of the Gospel than you did before: forsomuch as your Grace's favour to the gospel was not led by affection unto her, but by zeal unto the truth. And thus I beseech Almighty God, whose gospel he hath ordained your Grace to be defender of, ever to preserve your Grace from all evil, and give you at the end the promise of his Gospel.

Letter to King Henry VIII concerning Queen Catherine Howard (November 1541)

Cranmer not only told the King of his Queen's sexual indiscretions; he also confronted Catherine Howard herself, and was finally the confidant to whom she tearfully admitted the extent of her guilt. This letter, written of a subsequent interview, indicates both her frail mental health once she knew she was doomed, and his firm but committed pastoral care of her, when such attentions were not strictly necessary any longer. This letter survives in the Archbishop's own handwriting, an urgent, compassionate communication in the midst of extreme distress and crisis. Catherine was beheaded in February of 1542.

It may please your Majesty to understand, that at my repair unto the Queen's Grace, I found herein such lamentation and heaviness, as I never saw no creature; so that it would have pitied any man's heart in the world to have looked upon her; and in that vehement rage she continued, as they informed me which be about her, from my departure from her unto my return again; and then I found her, as I do suppose, far entered toward a frenzy, which I feared before my departure from her at my first being with her; and surely, if your Grace's comfort had not come in time, she could have continued no long time in that condition without a frenzy, which, nevertheless, I do yet much suspect to follow hereafter.

And as for my message from your Majesty unto her, I was purposed to enter communication in this wise; first, to exaggerate the grievousness of her demerits; then to declare unto her the justice of your Grace's laws, and what she ought to suffer by the same; and last of all to signify unto her your most gracious mercy: but when I saw in what condition she was, I was fain to turn my purpose, and to begin at the last part first, to comfort her by your Grace's benignity and mercy; for else the recital of your Grace's laws, with the aggravation of her offences, might, peradventure, have driven her unto some dangerous ecstasy, and else into a very frenzy; so that the words of comfort coming last might peradventure have come too late. And after I had declared your Grace's mercy extended unto her, she held up her hands and gave most humble thanks unto your Majesty, who had showed unto her more grace and mercy, than she herself thought meet to sue for or could have hoped of; and then, for a time, she began to be more temperate and quiet, saving that she still sobbed and wept; but after a little pausing she suddenly fell into a new rage, much worse than she was before.

Now I do use her thus; when I do see her in any such extreme brayds,[19] I do travail with her to know the cause, and then, as much as I can, I do labour to take away, or at the least to mitigate the cause; and so I did at that time. I told her there was some new fantasy come into her head, which I desired her to open unto me; and after a certain time, when she had recovered herself that she might speak, she cried and said, 'Alas, my lord, that I am alive, the fear of death grieved me not so much before, as doth now the remembrance of the King's goodness; for when I remember how gracious and loving a Prince I had, I cannot but sorrow; but this sudden mercy, and more than I could have looked for, showed unto me, so unworthy at this time, maketh mine offences to appear before mine eyes much more heinous than they did before: and the more I consider the greatness of his mercy, the more I do sorrow in my heart that I should so misorder myself against his Majesty.' And for any thing that I could say unto her, she continued in a great pang a long while, but after that

---

19 'emotional outbursts'.

she began something to remit her rage and come to herself, she was meetly well until night, and I had very good communication with her, and, as I thought, had brought her unto a great quietness.

Nevertheless, at night, about six of the clock, she fell into another like pang, but not so outrageous as the first was; and that was, as she showed me, for the remembrance of the time; for about that time, as she said, Master Hennage was wont to bring her knowledge of your Grace.

And because I lack time to write all things unto your Majesty, I have referred other things to be opened by the mouth of this bearer, Sir John Dudlay . . .

After weathering the storms of the 1540s, plots against his own life and efforts to separate him from the King and his favour, Thomas Cranmer was ultimately summoned by Henry to keep him company as he died. The King wanted no-one with him in his last earthly minutes but the man whose loyal devotion and prayerful presence had been a constant foundation of the previous 15 years and, by their constancy, therefore a rarity in his reign. On 28 January 1547, Cranmer as the King's friend and chaplain entered the royal bedchamber to find his master close to death. John Foxe later recorded an account of the final moments of Henry's life, which brought to the fore Cranmer's gracious pastoral presence and gentle human warmth.

Then the archbishop, exhorting him to put his trust in Christ, and to call upon his mercy, desired him, though he could not speak, yet to give some token with his eyes or with his hand, that he trusted in the Lord. Then the King, holding him with his hand, did wring his hand in his as hard as he could.

Calling this 'the most long-lasting relationship of love which either man had known', MacCulloch well illustrates the tenderness and trust which could underlie the tension and frequent upheaval of life in Henry's court.[20] Cranmer, easing Henry's passage from the world without old traditions such as last rites or final anointing, would have reflected on how much religious change had taken root in England, but also how much more reform, in his mind, was yet needed. Before we examine the extraordinary changes of the reign of Edward VI, however, we shall need to see their roots in such evangelical projects of reform

---

20 MacCulloch, *Thomas Cranmer*, p. 360.

as Cranmer had managed to accomplish, in the often difficult and ever changing religious environment of Henrician England. To two of his most cherished goals, making the Bible in English more widely available and beginning to produce and instil reformed English versions of the liturgy, we now turn.

2

Exhorting the People: Bible and Prayer under Henry VIII

The Bible and liturgy in English

In common with other evangelicals and with the reforming humanist circles of Europe both Catholic and Protestant, Thomas Cromwell and Thomas Cranmer held as a basic and urgent requirement of a Christian nation that the Bible needed to be translated into the local language, and widely available. During the 1530s, when their cause was in the ascendancy, both men but especially Cromwell laboured hard to have an English Bible published and endorsed by royal command. The King himself seems to have been lukewarm about the project at best and later, in the more conservative 1540s, restricted popular access to the Bible. In 1537, Cromwell won from the King an agreement to license a new translation of the Bible in English for general use. In fact, the so-called 'Matthew' Bible in question was largely based on the controversial work of William Tyndale, but its authorization was a cause of huge delight to Cranmer.

The project of producing a new Bible, and of ensuring its placement in every English parish, took slightly longer. In April 1539, the 'Great Bible' finally appeared, complete with careful iconography, depicting the Archbishop at the King's right hand, receiving from his monarch the Word of God and faithfully disseminating it among the English people. Ironically, Thomas Cromwell's enemies began closing in on him, roused by years of his bullying in ecclesiastical and other affairs, even as the Bible, a vital symbol of the advance of evangelical priorities, went into a second edition the following year. The Reformation in England lost its greatest patron and prime mover just as it secured a vital advance. That second edition included a new Preface, written by Cranmer, on the use of the Bible, a feature that has sometimes led the Great Bible to be referred to as 'Cranmer's Bible', despite his own minimal role in its production.

Reprinted here are two documents: a letter written by Cranmer to Cromwell in 1537 indicating his joy at the news of an authorized

English Bible and his Preface to the second edition of the Great Bible, a classic and eloquent statement about Scripture and devotion, much admired at the time and much quoted since. It draws for its inspiration and authority both on the works of the ancient theologians of the Church, a common Protestant technique to show that the new faith was in fact a rescuing of pristine Christianity from the muddle and corruption of centuries of Roman Catholic accretions, and on the works of Christian humanist reformers such as Erasmus in stressing the Bible's unique status as the most precious and indeed only useful 'relic' which Christians possess. Cranmer's rather stern ending, too, reflects the seriousness of his purpose and his rock-firm conviction of the need both for wide readership of the Bible and for an end to upheaval and dispute in the Church.

My very singular and especial good Lord, in my most hearty wise I commend me to your Lordship. These shall be to give you my most hearty thanks that any heart can think, and that in the name of them all which favoureth God's word, for your diligence at this time in procuring the King's Highness to set forth the said God's word, and his Gospel, by his Grace's authority. For the which act, not only the King's Majesty, but also you shall have a perpetual laud and memory of all them that be now, or hereafter shall be God's faithful people, and the favourers of his word. And this deed you shall hear of at the great day, when all things shall be opened and made manifest. For our Saviour Christ saith in the said Gospel, that whosoever shrinketh from him and his word, and is abashed to profess and set it forth before men in this world, He will refuse him at that day: and contrary, whosoever constantly doth profess Him and his word, and studieth to set that forward in this world, Christ will declare the same at the last day before his Father and all his angels, and take upon him the defence of those men.[1]

Preface to the Bible of 1540

For two sundry sorts of people, it seemeth much necessary that something be said in the entry of this book, by the way of a preface or prologue: whereby after, it may be both the better accepted of them

---

1 Thomas Cranmer, *The Remains of Thomas Cranmer*, 4 vols, ed. Henry Jenkins (Oxford: Oxford University Press, 1833), vol. 1, pp. 199–201.

which hitherto could not well bear it, and also the better used of them which heretofore have misused it. For truly some there are, that be too slow and need the spur; some other seem too quick and need more of the bridle. Some lose their game by shortshooting, some by overshooting. Some walk too much on the left hand; some too much on the right. In the former sort be all they, that refuse to read or hear read, the Scripture in the vulgar tongue, much worse they that also let, or discourage the other from the reading or hearing thereof. In the latter sort be they, which by their inordinate reading, undiscreet speaking, contentious disputing, or otherwise by their licentious living, slander and hinder the word of God most of all other, whereof they would seem to be greatest furtherers. These two sorts, albeit they be most far unlike the one to the other, yet they both deserve in effect like reproach. Neither can I well tell, whether of them I may judge the more offender, him that doth obstinately refuse so godly and goodly knowledge, or him that so ungodly and so ungoodly doth abuse the same.

And as touching the former, I would marvel much, that any man should be so mad, as to refuse in darkness, light; in hunger, food; in cold, fire. For the word of God is light . . . food . . . fire . . . I would marvel, I say, at this, save that I consider, how much custom and usage may do. So that if there were a people, as some writ . . . which never saw the sun, by reason that they be situated far toward the North Pole, and be enclosed and overshadowed with high mountains; it is credible and like enough, that if by the power and will of God the mountains should sink down, and give place that the light of the sun might have entrance to them, at the first some of them would be offended therewith. And the old proverb affirmeth, that after tillage of corn was first found, many delighted more to feed of mast and acorns, wherewith they had been accustomed, and to be offended with all things thereto contrary. And therefore I can well think them worthy pardon, which at the coming abroad of Scripture doubted and drew back. But such as will persist still in their wilfulness, I must needs judge not only foolish, froward, and obstinate, but also peevish, perverse, and indurate.

And yet, if the matter should be tried by custom, we might also allege custom for the reading of the Scripture in the vulgar tongue, and prescribe the more ancient custom. For it is not much above one hundred years ago, since Scripture hath not been accustomed to be read in the vulgar tongue within this realm: and many hundred years before that, it was translated and read in the Saxons' tongue, which at that time was our mother's tongue; whereof there remaineth yet divers copies, found lately in old abbeys, of such antique manners of writing and speaking, that few men now been able to read and understand them. And when this language waxed old and out of common usage, by cause folk should not lack the fruit of reading, it was again translated into the newer language, whereof yet also many copies remain and be daily found.

Cranmer here offers a lengthy quotation from the fourth-century bishop John Chrysostom on the importance of lay people reading the Bible in their own language.

Now if I should in like manner bring forth what the self-same doctor speaketh in other places, and what other doctors and writers say concerning the same purpose, I might seem to you to write another Bible, rather than to make a preface to the Bible. Wherefore in a few words to comprehend the largeness and utility of the Scripture, how it containeth fruitful instruction and erudition for every man; if any thing be necessary to be learned, of the holy Scripture we may learn it. If falsehood shall be reproved, thereof we may gather wherewithal. If any thing be to be corrected or amended, if there need any exhortation of consolation, of the Scripture we may well learn. In the Scriptures be the fat pastures of the soul; therein is no venomous meat, no unwholesome thing; they be the very dainty and pure feeding. He that is ignorant shall find there what he should learn. He that is a perverse sinner shall there find his damnation, to make him tremble for fear. He that laboureth to serve God shall find there his glory, and the promises of eternal life, exhorting him more diligently to labour. Herein may princes learn how to govern their subjects: subjects, obedience love and dread to their princes. Husbands how they should behave them unto their wives, how to educate their children and servants; and contrary, the wives, children and servants may know their duty to their husbands, parents and masters. Here may all manner of persons, men, women, young, old, learned, unlearned, rich, poor, priests, laymen, lords, ladies, officers, tenants, and mean men, virgins, wives, widows, lawyers, merchants, artificers, husbandmen and all manner of persons of what estate or condition soever they be, may in this book learn all things what they ought to believe, what they ought to do, as well concerning Almighty God, as also concerning themselves and all other. Briefly, to the reading of the Scripture none can be enemy, but that either be so sick, that they love not to hear of any medicine; or else that be so ignorant, that they know not Scripture to be the most healthful medicine.

Therefore as touching this former part, I will here conclude, and take it as a conclusion sufficiently determine and appoint, that it is convenient and good the Scripture to be read of all sorts and kinds of people, and in the vulgar tongue, without further allegations and probations for the same; which shall not need, since that this one place of John Chrysostom is enough and sufficient to persuade all them that be not frowardly and perversely set in their own wilful opinion. Specially now that the King's Highness, being supreme head next under Christ of this church of England, hath approved with his royal assent the setting forth hereof. Which only to all true and obedient subjects ought to be a sufficient reason for the allowance of the same, without farther delay, reclamation, or resistance, although there were no preface, nor other reason herein expressed.

Therefore now to come to the second and latter part of my purpose. Here is nothing so good in this world but it may be abused, and turned from fruitful and wholesome to hurtful and noisome. What is there above, better than the sun, the moon, the stars? Yet was there, that took occasion, by the great beauty and virtue of them, to dishonour God, and to defile themselves with idolatry, giving the honour of the living God and Creator of all things to such things as he had created. What is there here beneath, better than fire, water, meats, drinks, metals of gold, silver, iron and steel? Yet we see daily great harm and much mischief done by every one of these, as well for lack of wisdom and providence of them that suffer evil, as by the malice of them that worketh the evil. Thus to them that be evil of themselves, every thing setteth forward and increaseth their evil, be it of his own nature a thing never so good. Like as contrarily to them that studieth and endeavoureth themselves to goodness, every thing prevaileth them, and profiteth unto good, be it of his own nature a thing never so bad. As St. Paul saith, *His, qui diligunt Deum, omnia cooperantur in bonum.*[2] Even as out of most venomous worms is made treacle,[3] the most sovereign medicine for the preservation of man's health in time of danger. Wherefore I would advise you all that cometh to the reading or hearing of this book, which is the word of

---

2 Romans 8.28: 'All things work together for good for those who love God.'

3 The origin of our word 'treacle' is in fact this medicine or ointment; the version Cranmer here describes is only one of a number of similar treatments known in his day.

God, the most precious jewel and most holy relic that remaineth on earth, that ye bring with you the fear of God, and that ye do it with all reverence, and use your knowledge thereof not to vainglory of frivolous disputation, but to the honour of God, increase of virtue, and edification both of yourselves and other.

Cranmer changes sources here, to quote at length the work of the fourth-century theologian Gregory of Nazianzus, referring to the unnecessary and in his view frivolous disputations about the Bible which were consuming the Christians of his day.

Hitherto have I recited the mind of Gregory Nazianzene in that book which I spake of before.[4] The same author sayeth also in another place, 'that the learning of a Christian man ought to begin of the fear of God, to end in matters of high speculation: and not contrarily to begin with speculation, and to end in fear. For speculation', sayeth he, 'either high cunning and knowledge, if it be not stayed with the bridle of fear to offend God, is dangerous, and enough to tumble a man headlong down the hill. Therefore,' sayeth he, 'the fear of God must be the first beginning, and as it were an A.B.C. or an introduction to all them that shall enter to the very true and most fruitful knowledge of holy Scriptures. Where as is the fear of God, there is,' sayeth he, 'the keeping of the Commandments, there is the cleansing of the flesh; which flesh is a cloud before the souls eye, and suffereth it not purely to see the beam of the heavenly light. Where as is the cleansing of the flesh, there is the illumination of the Holy Ghost, the end of all our desires, and the very light whereby the verity of Scripture is seen and perceived.' This is the mind and almost the words of Gregory Nazianzene, doctor of the Greek church; of whom St. Jerome sayeth, that unto his time the Latin church had no writer able to be compared, and to make an even match with him.

Therefore to conclude this latter part; every man that cometh to the reading of this holy book ought to bring with him first and foremost this fear of Almighty God; and then next, a firm and stable purpose to reform his own self according thereunto; and so to continue, proceed and prosper from time to time, shewing himself to be a sober and fruitful hearer and learner. Which if he do, he shall prove at length well able to teach, though not with his mouth, yet with his living and good example; which is sure the most lively and effectuous

---

4 His *De Theologia*, Book One.

form and manner of teaching. He that otherwise intermeddleth with this book, let him be assured that once he shall make account therefore, when he shall have said to him, as it is written in the prophet David, 'Unto the ungodly said God: Why dost thou preach my laws, and takest my testament in thy mouth? Whereas thou hatest to be reformed: and hast been partaker with advoutrers.[5] Thou hast let thy mouth speak wickedness: and with thy tongue thou hast set forth deceit. Thou satest, and spakest against thy brother: and hast slandered thine own mother's son. These things hast thou done, and I held my tongue, and thou thoughtest wickedly, that I am even such a one as thyself: but I will reprove thee, and set before thee the things that thou hast done. O consider this ye that forget God: lest I pluck you away, and there be none to deliver you. Whoso offereth me thanks and praise, he honoureth me: and to him that ordereth his conversation right will I show the salvation of God.'[6]

God save the King.

The Great Bible was the high-water mark of the efforts of the reforming party to widen access to Scripture under Henry VIII. The power of its iconography, the momentous import of its making Scripture available in English widely for the first time, and the strength of Cranmer's endorsement and instruction were major religious events in the realm. As we have seen, however, this vital evangelical document was being created and disseminated even as those driving the project lost energy and influence, as the tragic but perhaps inevitable demise of Cromwell unfolded. Cranmer fought bravely, amid the convulsions and confusions of the early 1540s, to protect and preserve the Bible and its availability to as many as possible, and he did so rather successfully. Even so, the view of the *King's Book* in 1543 was once more that the Bible was to to be read by and interpreted only by the learned and priestly, and the Archbishop must have mourned what he would have viewed as the loss of ground, and the denial of truth, which this position represented.[7]

Through the latter years of Henry's reign, Cranmer dabbled in a number of projects of liturgical revision and translation which prefigured

---

5 Adulterers.

6 Psalm 50.

7 Diarmaid MacCulloch, *Thomas Cranmer* (New Haven and London: Yale University Press, 1996), pp. 238–40, 258–60; Christopher Haigh, *English Reformations* (Oxford: Oxford University Press, 1993), pp. 156 and 161.

his subsequent and extraordinary achievements in the *Book of Common Prayer*. Such endeavours reflected his tenacious ongoing reform efforts in the face of renewed conservative influence and the heightened authority of Stephen Gardiner and others.[8] As part of the drive for religious uniformity in England, and under that guise, the Archbishop worked on new editions of the litany, which was a penitential solemn procession with intercession, and the breviary, a collection of prayers for private use at the traditional eight offices through the day. It was thus in the mid-1540s that Cranmer first attempted to reduce the daily offices to two, Matins and Evensong, as he was finally to do under Edward VI with the Prayer Book: but the breviary revision came to naught, until material from it finally found its way from Cranmer's notebooks to the Edwardian Prayer Books. The new litany was published in 1544, prefaced with an *Exhortation Unto Prayer* written by Cranmer, which is thus one of his first published homilies. The *Exhortation* is reproduced in full below, a basic but eloquent model sermon to be preached at times of common prayer, outlining the Archbishop's first thoughts on an institution that was to become so firmly his own creation.

Forasmuch as prayer is the very true mean, ordained of Almighty God, and taught us plainly in his holy word, whereby not only we may, but also by God's holy commandment be bounden to have a recourse, and a refuge, for help and aid of Almighty God, our heavenly Father, not only in all our necessities, and tribulations of this world, but also universally in all our affairs and businesses, whatsoever shall befall unto us, or else whatsoever thing we shall enterprize or take in hand: and forasmuch also, as our Father in heaven, of his mere mercy and infinite goodness, hath bounden himself by his own free promise, and certified us of the same by his own Son, our only Saviour and Lord Christ Jesu in his gospel, that, whatsoever we shall ask of him, we shall have it, so that we ask such things, and in such sort, as we ought to do: for these causes, good Christian people, being thus grounded upon the sure foundation of God's holy and blessed word, which cannot deceive us, we are here at this time gathered together, to make our common prayer to our heavenly Father. But now, good Christian people, that by the true use of prayer we may obtain and enjoy his gracious promise of aid, comfort and consolation, in all our affairs and necessities, two things concerning prayer are specially to

8 See Eamon Duffy, *The Stripping of the Altars* (New Haven and London: Yale University Press, 1992), p. 443.

be learned. The first is, to know for what things we ought to make our request, and petition in our prayer: the second is, in what wise we should make our prayer, in such sort as it may be acceptably heard and graciously granted of our heavenly Father.

As for the first, we ought instantly[9] to ask of our heavenly Father his holy and blessed Spirit, godly wisdom, faith, charity, and to fear and dread him, and that his holy name in all things and every where through all the whole world may be glorified; that his kingdom may come unto us, that is to say, that here he may reign in us by the faith of his well-beloved Son, our Saviour Jesus Christ, and after this life also to reign in us, and over us, everlastingly in glory.

We ought to pray, that his blessed will may be fulfilled here in this world among us, his mortal creatures, as it is of his immortal angels, and of all the holy company of the heavenly spirits. We must pray for our daily bread, that is, for our necessary food and sustenance both of body and soul: of body, as meat, drink and necessary apparel, peace, health, and whatsoever God knoweth to be necessary for the behoof and conservation of the same; that we may do to our Lord God true service therewith, every man in his state and vocation, whereunto God hath called him: of the soul, as the word of God, and the true knowledge of the same, the true conservation of our heavenly Father's holy and blessed sacraments, the lively bread and blessed body of our Saviour Jesu Christ, the holy and sacrate cup of the precious and blessed blood, which was shed for us upon the cross, to purchase us pardon and forgiveness of our sins.[10] Furthermore, we must pray for forgiveness of our sins, that our heavenly Father will be merciful unto us, and forgive us our sins, both many and great, whereby we offend against his infinite goodness, as we do forgive the offences of them that offend us; which, how great soever they appear unto us, yet, in comparison of the offences that we do against God, they be both small and few. We must pray, that our heavenly Father suffer us not to be led into temptation; for without his continual aid and protection we are but weak, and soon overthrown. Our ghostly enemy is strong, violent, fierce subtle and exceeding cruel. And, therefore, we must continually pray with all instance, that in all his assaults we may be delivered by the mighty hand of our heavenly Father from all

---

9 In the English of Cranmer's day: 'urgently', 'earnestly'.

10 We might note that the language used of the Eucharist was still very traditional in 1544, a reflection of the King's conservatism and the Archbishop's as yet unreformed theology: soon to evolve dramatically.

evil. Finally, and before all things, as St. Paul exhorteth us in the first epistle to Timothy, let us make our prayers and supplications, rendering and giving of thanks for all men; and namely, for kings, princes, and all other set in chief dignity and high rooms, that by their godly governance, their true, faithful and diligent execution of justice and equity unto all their subjects, our heavenly Father may be glorified, the commonwealth may be daily promoted and increased, and that we all, that are their subjects, may live in peace and quietness, with all godliness and virtue, and Christian princes and heads in unity and concord among themselves, ever calling upon their heavenly Father, which is the King of all kings and the Lord of all lords, which shall judge, without respect of persons, according to every man's doing or works; at whose hand the weak shall take no wrong, nor the mighty may not by any power escape his just judgement: that our princes, I say, thus calling upon their heavenly Father for grace, may ever in all their affairs be directed and governed by the Holy Spirit of God, and both rule and be ruled by his holy fear, to their own endless joy, comfort and consolation, and to their own everlasting salvation through our Saviour Jesus Christ.

And here, specially let us pray for our most dear and sovereign lord, the King's majesty, who doth not only study and care daily and hourly for our prosperity and wealth, but also spareth not to spend his substance and treasure, yea, ready at all times to endanger himself, for the tender love and fatherly zeal, that he beareth toward this his realm and the subjects of the same: who at this present time hath taken upon him the great and dangerous affairs of war.[11] Let us pray, that it may please Almighty God, Lord of hosts, in whose hands is only wealth and victory, mercifully to assist him, sending his holy angels to be his succour, keeper, and defender from all his adversaries, and from all evils. Let us pray for our brethren, that bend themselves to battle for God's cause and our defence, that God may grant them prosperous success, to our comfort, and the increase of his glory. Let us pray for ourselves, that remain at home, the Almighty God defend us from sin, sickness, dearth, and all other adversities of body and soul.

The second thing to be learned concerning prayer, is to know, how we shall make true prayer, so that it may be graciously heard, and mercifully granted, of our heavenly Father. First of all, we must, upon consideration of our heavenly Father's mercy and goodness towards us, and of his everlasting truth and free promise made unto us in

---

11 In 1544, Henry had launched attacks on both Scotland and France.

his own holy word, conceive a full affiance, hope and trust; and that, without wavering or doubtful mistrusting, either in his truth, his goodness, or in his almighty power; certainly assuring ourself, that both of his omnipotency he may do whatsoever shall please his goodness, and also for his infinite goodness and fatherly affection towards us that he will both hear and grant all our lawful and godly requests after that measure, sort and degree, as he, of his infinite and incomprehensible wisdom, knoweth the thing to be most meet, most convenient, and behooffull, both for his own glory and honour, and for the profit, behoof, and commodity of us his children.

Furthermore also it is necessarily required to that, that our prayer may be acceptable unto our heavenly Father, to have charity and brotherly love betwixt neighbour and neighbour, and towards all our even Christians. So Christ himself teacheth us, saying, 'When you stand to pray, forgive, if you have any displeasure against any person; that your Father, which is in heaven, may forgive you'. It is a true saying, that St. Augustine saith: 'There is no good fruit, no good deed, no good work, which springeth not out of the root of charity.' And St. Paul teacheth plainly, that where as charity lacketh, nothing can avail us.

And, moreover, we must in our prayer beware of vain glory and praise of man, outwardly showing a great pretence of holiness, and being vain of true godliness inwardly, only to have the commendation of men before the world; for, if we so do, we shall lose the reward and benefit of our prayer, as our Saviour Christ hath said his ownself. We must take heed, also, that we think not the virtue of prayer to consist in multiplying of many words, without faith and godly devotion, thinking, as the heathen doth, that for our many words, or much speaking, we shall be heard of our heavenly Father. Whosoever doth think so, he shall deceive himself; for God doth not regard neither the sweet sound of our voice, nor the great number of our words, but the earnest ferventness and true faithful devotion of our hearts. Finally, we must beware in our prayer of that common pestilent infection, and venomful poison, of all good prayer, that it is to say, when our mouth prayeth, and our hearts pray not: of the which the prophet Isaiah complaineth sore; and our Saviour, in St Matthew's gospel, rebuketh the Pharisees for the same, saying thus, 'O hypocrites, Isaiah the prophet prophesied well upon you, when he said thus, "This people draweth nigh me with their lips, but their hearts are far from me"'; that is to say, they speak with their tongue and lips the words of prayer, but in their heart they mind nothing less than they speak, as that the goodness of the prayer stood in the outward speaking only of the word, and not in the inward, true, and faithful request of the heart. And to the intent, therefore, your heart and lips may go together in prayer, it is very convenient, and much acceptable to God, that you should use your private prayer in your mother tongue, that you, understanding what you ask of God, may more earnestly and fervently desire the same, your hearts and minds agreeing to your mouth and words. Wherefore, let us eschew, good people, in our prayers all the afore-rehearsed vices; for else we shall not obtain our petitions and requests, but, contrariwise, we shall highly displease God, and grievously offend him. Therefore, good Christian brethren, seeing we are come together to pray, let us do it according to our bounden duty, and as it ought to be done. Let us truly pray with a faithful heart, and a sure affiance of our heavenly Father's infinite mercy, grace and goodness. Let us make our prayers, being in love and charity with all, and every one, of our neighbours; ever having in our heart an earnest request and desire of those godly benefits, which are appointed in God's word, that we should pray for; and yet, not prescribing unto God either the time, place, measure or degree, of his gracious benefits, but wholly committing ourselves to his blessed will and pleasure, receiving in good worth, and with thanksgiving, whatsoever, and whensoever, it shall please his gracious goodness to bestow his gracious gifts upon us. Let us also furnish and beautify this our prayer, that it may please God the better, and delight the ears of our heavenly Father, with fasting and wholesome abstinence, not only from all delicious living in voluptuous fare, and from all excesses of meat and drink, but also to chastise and kill the sinful lusts of the body, to make it bow, and ready to obey, unto the spiritual motions of the Holy Ghost. Let us also furnish it with almsdeed, and with works of mercy and charity: for prayer is good and acceptable unto God, when it is accompanied with almsdeeds, and with the works of mercy, as the holy man Toby saith; with the which, and using the virtues afore rehearsed, and also eschewing diligently the aforesaid vices, our prayers shall be of much price and value, as was the prayers of Eli, Daniel and Moses, before our heavenly Father, and that, for our Saviour Jesus Christ's sake, which hath redeemed us with his precious blood, and hath signed and sealed us up to everlasting life. To whom, both now and ever, with his Father, and the Holy Ghost, be glory and honour without end. Amen.[12]

---

12 William Keating Clay, *Private Prayers, put forth by authority during the Reign of Queen Elizabeth* (Cambridge: University Press, 1851), pp. 565–70.

In 1545, the King published a primer, to encourage uniformity of private devotion across the land. We must assume that the Archbishop had a prime and guiding role in its production: such features as its reduction of the number of saints' days, and its curtailment of prayer for the dead and to the Blessed Sacrament certainly point to his influence and involvement. His confession that his poetic efforts lacked 'the grace and facility that I would wish they had' was proved justified by his attempts to translate Latin hymns into English[13] and we pass over them here to preserve his modesty. Excerpted below are a few elements of the 1545 primer: a grace to be said before dinner, which already showcases the Archbishop's fluency; the 1544 litany, which was reproduced in the primer and strongly reflects the King's desire for uniformity and unity, so passionately shared by his Archbishop; one of the prayers on the Passion which seem to be by Cranmer himself, and which, in their beauty and thoughtfulness prefigure his later liturgical work. They also can be seen to prefigure, with dramatic and uncanny foresight, his own terrible passion of the 1550s. Finally, prayers on other occasions, part of the varied selection appended to the book for private and family use. We pass over for now the translations of liturgical texts – the prayer of John Chrysostom, *Te Deum, Magnificat, Nunc Dimittis* – which appeared here for the first time but were later used without further change in the Prayer Book.

A Grace

O Lord Jesus Christ, without whom nothing is sweet or savory; we beseech thee to bless us and our supper, and with thy blessed presence to cheer our hearts, that in all our meats and drinks, we may taste and savour of thee, to thy honour and glory. Amen.

The Litany (excerpt)

That it may please thee to illuminate all bishops, pastors and ministers of the Church, with true knowledge and understanding of thy word and that both by their preaching and living they may set forth and show it accordingly;
We beseech thee to hear us good Lord.
That it may please thee to bless and keep all thy people;
We beseech thee to hear us good Lord.

---

13 MacCulloch, *Thomas Cranmer*, p. 331.

That it may please thee to give to all nations unity, peace and concord;
We beseech thee to hear us good Lord.
That it may please thee to give us an heart to love and dread thee, and diligently to live after thy commandments;
We beseech thee to hear us good Lord.
That it may please thee to give all thy people increase of grace, to hear meekly thy word, and to receive it with pure affection, and to bring forth the fruits of the Spirit;
We beseech thee to hear us good Lord.
That it may please thee to bring into the way of truth all such as have erred, and are deceived;
We beseech thee to hear us good Lord.
That it may please thee to strengthen such as do stand; and to comfort and help the weak-hearted; and to raise up them that fall; and finally, to beat down Satan under our feet;
We beseech thee to hear us good Lord.
That it may please thee to succour, help and comfort all that be in danger, necessity, and tribulation;
We beseech thee to hear us good Lord.
That it may please thee to preserve all that travel by land or by water, all women labouring of child, all sick persons, and young children; and to show thy pity upon all prisoners and captives;
We beseech thee to hear us good Lord.
That it may please thee to defend, and provide for, the fatherless children, and widows, and all that be desolate and oppressed;
We beseech thee to hear us good Lord.
That it may please thee to have mercy upon all men;
We beseech thee to hear us good Lord.
That it may please thee to forgive our enemies, persecutors and slanderers, and to turn their hearts;
We beseech thee to hear us good Lord.
That it may please thee to give to our use the kindly fruits of the earth, so as in due time we may enjoy them; and to preserve them;
We beseech thee to hear us good Lord.
That it may please thee to give us true repentance; to forgive us all our sins, negligences, and ignorances; and to endue us with the grace of thy Holy Spirit, to amend our lives according to thy holy word;
We beseech thee to hear us good Lord.
. . . O God, merciful Father, that despisest not the sighing of a contrite heart, nor the desire of such as be sorrowful, mercifully assist

our prayers, that we make before thee in all our troubles and adversities, whensoever they oppress us. And graciously hear us, that those evils, which the craft and subtlety of the devil or man worketh against us, be brought to naught, and by the providence of thy goodness, they may be dispersed, that we thy servants, being hurt by no persecutions, may evermore give thanks unto thee, in thy holy Church, through Jesus Christ our Lord.

O Lord, arise, help us, and deliver us, for thy honour.

O God, we have heard with our ears, and our fathers have declared unto us, the noble works, that thou didst in their days, and in the old time before them.

O Lord, arise, help us, and deliver us for thy name's sake.

Glory to the Father the Son and the Holy Ghost, as it hath been from the beginning, is, and shall be ever world without end. **Amen.**

From our enemies defend us O Christ;

   Graciously look upon our afflictions.

Pitifully behold the dolour of our heart;

   Mercifully forgive the sins of thy people.

Favourably with mercy hear our prayers;

   O Son of David have mercy upon us.

Both now and ever vouchsafe to hear us O Christ;

   Graciously hear us O Christ: graciously hear us O Lord Christ.

A Prayer on the Passion (prefaced by five Psalms and John's account of the Passion)

Almighty God our heavenly Father we beseech thy gracious goodness, that likewise as thy only begotten and dearly beloved son our Saviour Jesus Christ according to his blessed will suffered willingly death and bitter passion for our redemption and salvation, having thereof foresight and certain knowledge: so in like manner, whensoever it shall be thy pleasure to lay like cross and affliction upon our backs, that we may also willingly and patiently bear it, to the true trial of our faith against the later day, and to thy everlasting glory, Hear us our heavenly Father for our Lord Jesus Christ's sake.

A Prayer at Your Uprising

O Lord Jesus Christ, which art the very bright sun of the world, ever rising, never falling, which with thy wholesome look engenderest, preservest, nourishest and makest joyful all things that are in heaven and in earth, shine favourably I beseech thee unto my spirit, that the night of sins and mists of errors driven away by thy inward light, I may walk all my life without stumbling and offence, comely as the day time, being pure from the works of darkness. Grant this O Lord which livest and reignest with the Father and the Holy Ghost for evermore. Amen.

A Prayer Before Ye Go To Bed

O Lord, which art only God, true gracious and merciful, which commandest them that love thy name to cast out fear and care from them, and to cast it on thee, promising most mercifully thyself to be their protector from their enemies, their refuge in danger, their governor in the day, their light in darkness and their watchman in the night also, never to sleep but to watch continually for the preserving of thy faithful: I beseech thee of thy bountiful goodness O Lord to forgive me wherein I have offended this day, and to receive me under thy protection this night, that I may rest in quietness both of body and soul. Grant mine eyes sleep, but let mine heart watch perpetually unto thee, that the weakness of the flesh cause me not to offend thee Lord, let me at all times feel thy goodness toward me, that I be at all times stirred to praise thee, late and early, and at midday thy praise be in my mouth, and at midnight, Lord instruct me in thy judgements that all the course of my life being led in holiness and purity I may be induct at last into the everlasting rest, which thou hast promised by thy mercy to them that obey thy word O Lord, to whom be honour praise and glory for ever. Amen.

3

Concord in Religion: Cranmer and Edward VI

The death of King Henry in January 1547, his Archbishop at his side, ushered in a short but vitally significant era of radical religious change in England. The evangelical group that had won the ascendancy at court in the critical final months of the old King's life soon swept away much of the traditional past and indelibly stamped their mark on the Church of England and its theological and liturgical character. Under the leadership of King Edward's uncle, Edward Seymour, as Protector, the Council acted swiftly to achieve their purposes. Cranmer, after the long, slow, difficult and often dangerous years under Henry, seems to have been especially ready to move forward with purpose and passion and exercised his archiepiscopal oversight and authority with renewed zeal. For all that, this purpose and passion were tempered with an insightful understanding of the times, prudent caution and a wise sense of the need to 'make haste slowly'.[1] As the young King's godfather, he also assumed an especially prominent role in furthering and encouraging Edward's already firm Protestant views during the six years of his reign. Cranmer wasted no time in making plain his and the Council's purpose and their determination that Edward himself would act as the figurehead and patron of their project, when he addressed the nation's peers and prelates, but in particular the infant monarch, amid the splendour of the coronation on 20 February 1547. Cranmer drew for a biblical model of kingship, not on David, but on Josiah, the Israelite king whose rediscovery of early scriptural texts in the Temple was said to have spurred his root-and-branch renewal of Jewish faith and practice in the seventh century BCE. It was the perfect evangelical example to choose, especially given that Josiah was also a child, aged only seven years, when he became king. This rousing speech, not only re-emphasizing the Royal Supremacy but also sternly advocating

---

1 See Introduction, pp. 11–15.

reform, represents one of the strongest of Cranmer's public oratorical offerings, articulate and impassioned.

Most Dread and Royal Sovereign: The Promises your Highness hath made here at your Coronation to forsake the Devil and all his works, are not to be taken in the Bishop of Rome's sense, when you commit anything distasteful to the see, to hit your Majesty in the teeth, as Pope Paul the third, late Bishop of Rome, sent to your royal father, saying, 'Didst thou not promise, at our permission of thy Coronation, to forsake the Devil and all his works, and dost thou turn to heresy? For the breach of this thy promise, knowest thou not, that it is in our power to dispose of thy sword and sceptre to whom we please?' We, your Majesty's clergy, do humbly conceive, that this promise reacheth not at your Highness' sword, spiritual or temporal, or in the least at your Highness swaying the sceptre of this your dominion, as you and your predecessors have had them from God. Neither could your ancestors lawfully resign up their crowns to the Bishops of Rome or his legates, according to their ancient oaths taken upon that ceremony.

The Bishops of Canterbury for the most part have crowned your predecessors, and anointed them kings of this land: yet it was not in their power to receive or reject them, neither did it give them authority to prescribe them conditions to take or to leave their crowns, although the Bishops of Rome would encroach upon your predecessors by his bishops' act and oil, that in the end they might possess those bishops with an interest to dispose of their crowns at their pleasure. But the wiser sort will look to their claws and clip them.

The solemn rites of Coronation have their ends and utility, yet neither direct force or necessity: they be good admonitions to put kings in mind of their duty to God, but no increasement of their dignity. For they be God's anointed, not in respect of the oil which the bishop useth, but in consideration of their power which is ordained, of their sword which is authorized, of their persons which are elected by God, and indued with the gifts of his Spirit, for the better ruling and guiding of his people. The oil, if added, is but a ceremony; if it be wanting, that king is yet a perfect monarch notwithstanding, and God's anointed, as well as if he were inoiled. Now for the person or bishop that doth anoint a king, it is proper to be done by the chiefest; but if they cannot, or will not, any bishop may perform this ceremony.

To condition with monarchs upon these ceremonies, the Bishop of Rome (or other bishops owning his supremacy) hath no authority:

but he may faithfully declare what God requires at the hands of kings and rulers, that is, religion and virtue. Therefore not from the Bishop of Rome, but as a messenger from my Saviour Jesus Christ, I shall most humbly admonish your Royal Majesty, what things your Highness is to perform.

Your Majesty is God's vicegerent and Christ's vicar within your own dominions, and to see, with your predecessor Josiah, God truly worshipped, and idolatry destroyed, the tyranny of the Bishops of Rome banished from your subjects, and images removed. These acts be signs of a second Josiah, who reformed the church of God in his days. You are to reward virtue, to revenge sin, to justify the innocent, to relieve the poor, to procure peace, to repress violence, and to execute justice throughout your realms. For precedents on those kings who performed not these things, the old law shows how the Lord revenged his quarrel; and on those kings who fulfilled these things, he poured forth his blessings in abundance. For example, it is written of Josiah in the book of the Kings thus; 'Like unto him there was no king before him, that turned to the Lord with all his heart, according to all the law of Moses, neither after arose there any like him.' This was to that prince a perpetual fame of dignity, to remain to the end of days.

Being bound by my function to lay these things before your Royal Highness, the one as a reward, if you fulfil, the other as a judgment from God, if you neglect them: yet I openly declare, before the living God, and before these nobles of the land, that I have no commission to denounce your Majesty deprived, if your Highness miss in part, or in whole, of these performances; much less to draw up indentures between God and your Majesty, or to say you forfeit your crown with a clause, for the Bishop of Rome, as have been done by your Majesty's predecessors, King John, and his son Henry of this land. The Almighty God of his mercy let the light of his countenance shine upon your Majesty, grant you a prosperous and happy reign, defend you and save you: and let your subjects say, 'Amen'. God save the King![2]

The Edwardian Homilies

In the summer of 1547, a series of injunctions was issued for a great visitation of the English parishes. The new regime was determined to

---

2 Thomas Cranmer, *The Remains of Thomas Cranmer*, 4 vols, ed. Henry Jenkins (Oxford: Oxford University Press, 1833), vol. 2, pp. 118–20.

begin its root-and-branch reform of religion with vigour and strength. A major part of the initiative was the publication of an official collection of homilies, prescribed to be read in all English parish churches. It is beyond reasonable doubt that, of the twelve homilies in the collection, Cranmer was the author of three, excerpts from which follow. The first, on salvation, revisits the vital theme of justification which had been such a sticking point in the days of the old king; Cranmer here at last gives full vent to his theology of salvation and then follows it up with a further treatise on the primacy of faith in the believer's life. The content and tenor of these homilies infuriated traditionalists with their clear Lutheran bent: Cranmer's arch-opponent, Bishop Stephen Gardiner of Winchester, railed against them from his prison cell. Nothing, in fact, could have been more likely to confirm Cranmer in his words and opinions than Gardiner's displeasure; certainly, in these pieces we see the contours of overt Protestant thought and belief which was now the official position of the Church of England.

An Homily on the Salvation of Mankind, by only Christ our Saviour, from Sin and Death Everlasting

Because all men be sinners and offenders against God, and breakers of his law and commandments, therefore can no man by his own acts, works and deeds (seem they never so good) be justified and made righteous before God: but every man of necessity is constrained to seek for another righteousness or justification, to be received at God's own hands, that is to say, the remission, pardon and forgiveness of his sins and trespasses in such things as he hath offended. And this justification or righteousness, which we so receive by God's mercy and Christ's merits, embraced by faith, is taken, accepted, and allowed of God, for our perfect and full justification. For the more full understanding hereof, it is our parts and duty ever to remember the great mercy of God, how that (all the world being wrapped in sin by the breaking of the law) God sent his only son our saviour Christ into this world, to fulfil the law for us, and by shedding of his most precious blood to make a sacrifice and satisfaction, or (as it may be called) amends to his Father for our sins, to assuage his wrath and indignation conceived against us for the same.

Insomuch that infants being baptized, and dying in their infancy, are by this sacrifice washed from their sins, brought to God's favour, and made his children, and inheritors of his kingdom of heaven. And they which actually do sin after their baptism, when they convert and turn again to God unfeignedly, they are likewise washed by this sacrifice from their sins, in such sort, that there remaineth not any spot of sin that shall be imputed to their damnation.

[After a discussion of some passages of Paul in Romans, the texts so critical in Martin Luther's new understanding of justification:] In these foresaid places, the Apostle toucheth specially three things, which must concur and go together in our justification. Upon God's part, his great mercy and grace; upon Christ's part, justice, that is, the satisfaction of God's justice, or price of our redemption, by the offering of his body and shedding of his blood, with fulfilling of the law perfectly and thoroughly; and upon our part, true and lively faith in the merits of Jesu Christ, which yet is not ours, but by God's working in us. So that in our justification, is not only God's mercy and grace, but also his justice, which the apostle calleth the justice of God; and it consisteth in paying our ransom, and fulfilling of the law: and so the grace of God doth not exclude the justice of God in our justification, but only excludeth the justice of man, that is to say, the justice of our works, as to be merits of deserving our justification. And therefore St. Paul declareth here nothing upon the behalf of man concerning his justification, but only a true and lively faith, which nevertheless is the gift of God, and not man's only work without God.

And yet that faith doth not exclude repentance, hope, love, dread, and the fear of God, to be joined with faith in every man that is justified; but it excludeth them from the office of justifying. So that although they be all present together in him that is justified, yet they justify not altogether. Nor that faith also doth not exclude the justice of our good works, necessarily to be done afterward of our duty towards God; (for we are most bounden to serve God, in doing good deeds commanded by him in his holy scripture, all the days of our life;) but it excludeth them, so that we may not do them to this intent, to be made good by doing of them. For all the good works that we do be unperfect, and therefore not able to deserve our justification: but our justification doth come freely by the mere mercy of God, and of so great and free mercy, that whereas all the world was not able of themselves to pay any part towards their ransom, it pleased our heavenly Father of his infinite mercy, without any our desert or deserving, to prepare for us the most precious jewels of Christ's body and blood, whereby our ransom might be fully paid, the law fulfilled, and his justice fully satisfied. So that Christ is now the righteousness of all them that truly do believe in him. He for them paid their ransom by his death. He for them fulfilled the law in his life. So that now in him, and by him, every true Christian man may be called a fulfiller of the law; forasmuch as that which their infirmity lacketh, Christ's justice hath supplied.

[Characteristically, Cranmer continues to offer biblical and ancient theological sources further to bolster his claims:] Nevertheless, this sentence, that we be justified by faith only, is not so meant of them, that the said justifying faith is alone in man, without true repentance, hope, charity, dread, and the fear of God, at any time or season. Nor when they say, that we be justified freely, they mean not that we should or might afterward be idle, and that nothing should be required on our parts afterward. Neither they mean not so to be justified without good works, that we should do no good works at all, like as shall be more expressed at large hereafter. But this proposition, that we be justified by faith only, freely, and without works, is spoken for to take away clearly all merit of our works, as being insufficient to deserve our justification at God's hands, and thereby most plainly to express the weakness of man, and the goodness of God; the great infirmity of ourselves, and the might and power of God; the imperfectness of our own works, and the most abundant grace of our saviour Christ; and therefore wholly for to ascribe the merit and deserving of our justification unto Christ only, and his most precious blood-shedding. This faith the holy scripture teacheth; this is the strong rock and foundation of Christian religion; this doctrine all old and ancient authors of Christ's church do approve; this doctrine advanceth and setteth forth the true glory of Christ, and suppresseth the vain-glory of man; this whosoever denieth, is not to be reputed for a true Christian man, nor for a setter-forth of Christ's glory; but for an adversary of Christ and his gospel, and for a setter-forth of men's vain-glory.

I shall plainly and shortly so declare the right understanding of [the doctrine of justification by faith alone], that no man shall justly think that he may thereby take any occasion of carnal liberty to follow the desires of the flesh, or that thereby any kind of sin shall be committed, or any ungodly living the more used.

First, you shall understand, that in our justification by Christ it is not all one thing, the office of God unto man, and the office of man unto God. Justification is not the office of man, but of God; for man cannot justify himself by his own works, neither in part, nor in the whole; for that were the greatest arrogancy and presumption of man that Antichrist could erect against God, to affirm that a man might by his own works take away and purge his own sins, and so justify himself. But justification is the office of God only, and is not a thing which we render unto him, but which we receive of him; not which we give to him, but which we take of him, by his free mercy, and by the only merits of his most dearly beloved son, our only redeemer, saviour, and justifier, Jesus Christ. So that the true understanding of this doctrine, we be justified freely by faith without works, or that we be justified by faith in Christ only, is not, that this our own act to believe in Christ, or this our faith in Christ, which is within us, doth justify us, and merit our justification unto us; (for that were to count to ourselves to be justified by some act or virtue that is within ourselves;) but the true understanding and meaning thereof is, that although we hear God's word, and believe it; although we have faith, hope, charity, repentance, dread and fear of God within us, and do never so many good works thereunto; yet we must renounce the merit of all our said virtues, of faith, hope, charity and all our other virtues and good deeds, which we either have done, shall do, or can do, as things that be far too weak and insufficient and unperfect, to deserve remission of our sins, and our justification; and therefore we must trust only in God's mercy, and in that sacrifice which our high-priest and saviour Christ Jesus, the son of God, once offered for us upon the cross, to obtain thereby God's grace and remission, as well of our original sin in baptism, as of all actual sin committed by us after our baptism, if we truly repent, and convert unfeignedly to him again.

. . . Here you have heard the office of God in our justification, and how we receive it of him freely, by his mercy, without our deserts, through true and lively faith. Now you shall hear the office and duty of a Christian man unto God, what we ought on our part to render unto God again for his great mercy and goodness. Our office is, not to pass the time of this present life unfruitfully and idly, after that we are baptized or justified, not caring how few good works we do, to the glory of God, and profit of our neighbours: much less is it our office, after that we be once made Christ's members, to live contrary to the same; making ourselves members of the Devil, walking after his enticements, and after the suggestions of the world and the flesh, whereby we know that we do serve the world and the Devil, and not God. For that faith which bringeth forth (without repentance) either evil works, or no good works, is not a right, pure and lively faith, but a dead, devilish, counterfeit, and even feigned faith, as St. Paul and St. James call it. For even the devils know and believe that Christ was born of a virgin; that he fasted forty days and forty nights without meat and drink; that he wrought all kind of miracles, declaring himself very God: they believe also, that Christ for our sakes suffered most painful death, to redeem us from eternal death, and that he rose again from death the third day: they believe that he ascended into heaven, and that he sitteth on the right hand of the Father, and at the last end of this world shall come again, and judge both the quick and the dead. These articles of our faith the devils believe, and so they believe all things that be written in the New and Old Testament to be true: and yet for all this faith they be but devils, remaining still in their damnable estate, lacking the very true Christian faith.

For the right and true Christian faith is, not only to believe that holy Scripture, and all the foresaid articles of our faith are true; but also to have a sure trust and confidence in God's merciful promises, to be saved from everlasting damnation by Christ: whereof doth follow a loving heart to obey his commandments. And this true Christian faith neither any devil hath, nor yet any man, which in the outward profession of his mouth, and in his outward receiving of the sacraments, in coming to the church, and in all other outward appearances, seemeth to be a Christian man, and yet in his living and deeds showeth the contrary. For how can a man have this true faith, this sure trust and confidence in God, that by the merits of Christ his sins be remitted, and he reconciled to the favour of God, and to be partaker of the kingdom of heaven by Christ, when he liveth ungodly, and denieth Christ in his deeds? Surely no such ungodly man can have this faith and trust in God . . .

Therefore, to conclude, considering the infinite benefits of God, showed and exhibited unto us mercifully without our deserts, who hath not only created us of nothing, and from a piece of vile clay of his infinite goodness hath exalted us, as touching our soul, unto his own similitude and likeness; but also, whereas we were condemned to hell and death eternal, hath given his own natural son, being God eternal, immortal, and equal unto himself in power and glory, to be incarnated, and to take our mortal nature upon him, with the infirmities of the same, and in the same nature to suffer most shameful and painful death for our offences, to the intent to justify us, and to restore us to life everlasting: so making us also his dear beloved children, brethren unto his only son our saviour Christ, and inheritors for ever with him of his eternal kingdom of heaven: these great and merciful benefits of God, if they be well considered, do neither minister unto us occasion to be idle, and to live without doing any good works, neither yet stirreth us by any means to do evil things; but contrariwise, if we be not desperate persons, and our hearts harder than stones, they move us to render ourselves unto God wholly, with all our will, hearts, might and power, to serve him in all good deeds, obeying his commandments during our lives, to seek in all things his glory and honour, not our sensual pleasures and vain-glory; evermore dreading willingly to offend such a merciful God, and loving Redeemer, in word, thought, or deed. And the said benefits of God, deeply considered, do move us for his sake also to be ever ready to give ourselves to our neighbours, and, as much as lieth in us, to study with all our endeavour to do good to every man. These be the fruits of the true faith, to do good as much as lieth in us to every man, and, above all things, and in all things, to advance the glory of God, of whom only we have our sanctification, justification, salvation and redemption: to whom be ever glory, praise and honour, world without end. Amen.[3]

A Short Declaration of the True, Lively, and Christian Faith

The first entry unto God, good Christian people, is through faith, whereby (as it is declared in the last sermon) we be justified before God. And lest any man should be deceived for lack of right understanding hereof, it is diligently to be noted, that faith is taken in the Scripture two manner of ways. There is one faith, which in Scripture is called a dead faith, which bringeth forth no good works, but is idle, barren and unfruitful. And this faith, by the holy apostle St. James, is compared to the faith of devils, which believe God to be true and just, and tremble for fear; yet they do nothing well, but all evil. And such a manner of faith have the wicked and naughty Christian people, 'which confess God', as St. Paul saith, 'in their mouth', but 'deny him in their deeds, being abominable, and without the right faith, and in all good works reprovable'.[4] And this faith is a persuasion and belief in man's heart, whereby he knoweth that there is a God, and assenteth unto all truth of God's most holy word, contained in holy Scripture. So that it consisteth only in believing of the word of God, that it is true. And this is not properly called faith. But as he that readeth Caesar's Commentaries, believing the same to be true, hath thereby a knowledge of Caesar's life and noble acts, because he

---

3 Cranmer, *Remains*, vol. 2, pp. 138–50.
4 Biblical references here are to Jas. 2 and Titus 1.

believeth the history of Caesar: yet it is not properly said, that he believeth in Caesar, of whom he looketh for no help or benefit. Even so, he that believeth that all that is spoken of God in the Bible is true, and yet liveth so ungodly, that he cannot look to enjoy the promises and benefits of God; although it may be said, that such a man hath a faith and belief to the words of God; yet it is not properly said that he believeth in God, or hath such a faith and trust in God, whereby he may surely look for grace, mercy and eternal life at God's hand, but rather for indignation and punishment, according to the merits of his wicked life . . . This dead faith therefore is not that sure and substantial faith which saveth sinners.

Another faith there is in scripture, which is not, as the foresaid faith, idle, unfruitful, and dead, but 'worketh by charity' (as St. Paul declareth, Gal. 5) which as the other vain faith is called a dead faith, so may this be called a quick or lively faith. And this is not only the common belief of the articles of our faith, but it is also a sure trust and confidence of the mercy of God through our lord Jesus Christ, and a steadfast hope of all good things to be received at God's hand: and that although we, through infirmity, or temptation of our ghostly enemy, do fall from him by sin; yet if we return again unto him by true repentance, that he will forgive and forget our offences for his son's sake, our saviour Jesus Christ, and will make us inheritors with him of his everlasting kingdom; and that in the mean time, until that kingdom come, he will be our protector and defender in all perils and dangers, whatsoever do chance: and that though sometime he do send us sharp adversity, yet that evermore he will be a loving father unto us, correcting us for our sin, but not withdrawing his mercy finally from us, if we trust in him, and commit ourselves wholly to him, hang only upon him, and call upon him, ready to obey and serve him. This is the true, lively, and unfeigned Christian faith, and is not in the mouth and outward profession only, but it liveth, and stirreth inwardly in the heart. And this faith is not without hope and trust in God, nor without the love of God and of our neighbours, nor without the fear of God, nor without the desire to hear God's word, and to follow the same in eschewing evil, and doing gladly all good works.

[Cranmer goes on to note that there are three things which must be noted about true faith.] First, that this faith doth not lie dead in the heart, but is lively and fruitful in bringing forth good works. Second, that without it can no good works be done, that shall be acceptable and pleasant unto God. Third, what manner of good works they be that this faith doth bring forth.

For the first, as the light cannot be hid, but will show forth itself at one place or another; so a true faith cannot be kept secret; but when occasion is offered, it will break out, and show itself by good works. And as the living body of a man ever exerciseth such things as belongeth to a natural and living body, for nourishment and preservation of the same, as it hath need, opportunity, and occasion; even so the soul that hath a lively faith in it will be doing always some good work, which shall declare that it is living, and will not be unoccupied. Therefore, when men hear in the Scriptures so high commendations of faith, that it maketh us to please God, to live with God, and to be the children of God; if then they phantasy that they be set at liberty from doing all good works, and may live as they list, they trifle with God, and deceive themselves. And it is a manifest token that they be far from having the true and lively faith, and also far from knowledge what true faith meaneth. For the very sure and lively Christian faith is, not only to believe all things of God which are contained in holy Scripture, but also is an earnest trust and confidence in God, that he doth regard us, and hath cure of us, as the father of the child whom he doth love, and that he will be merciful unto us for his only son's sake, and that we have our saviour Christ our perpetual advocate and priest, in whose only merits, oblation and suffering, we do trust that our offences be continually washed and purged, whensoever we, repenting truly, do return to him with our whole heart, steadfastly determining with ourselves, through his grace, to obey and serve him in keeping his commandments, and never to turn back again to sin. Such is the true faith that the Scripture doth so much commend, the which, when it seeth and considereth what God hath done for us, is also moved, through continual assistance of the Spirit of God, to serve and please him, to keep his favour, to fear his displeasure, to continue his obedient children, showing thankfulness again by observing his commandments, and that freely, for true love chiefly, and not for dread of punishment, or love of temporal reward, considering how clearly, without our deservings, we have received his mercy and pardon freely.

There follows an extended survey of biblical passages which Cranmer cites as proof of his position. The homily concludes with a stirring peroration.

A man may soon deceive himself, and think in his own phantasy that he by faith knoweth God, loveth him, feareth him, and belongeth to him, when in very deed he doth nothing less. For the trial of all these things is a very godly and Christian life. He that feeleth his heart set to seek God's honour, and studieth to know the will and commandments of God, and to conform himself thereunto, and leadeth not his life after the desire of his own flesh to serve the devil by sin, but setteth his mind to serve God for God's own sake, and for his sake also to love all his neighbours, whether they be friends or adversaries, doing good to every man, as opportunity serveth, and willingly hurting no man: such a man may well rejoice in God, perceiving by the trade of his life, that he unfeignedly hath the right knowledge of God, a lively faith, a constant hope, a true and unfeigned love and fear of God. But he that casteth away the yolk of God's commandments from his neck, and giveth himself to live without true repentance, after his own sensual mind and pleasure, not regarding to know God's word, and much less to live according thereunto; such a man clearly deceiveth himself and seeth not his own heart, if he thinketh that he either knoweth God, loveth him, feareth him, or trusteth in him. Some peradventure phantasy in themselves that they belong to God, although they live in sin, and so they come to the church, and show themselves as God's dear children. But St. John saith plainly: 'If we say that we have any company with God, and walk in darkness, we do lie.' Other do vainly think that they know and love God, although they pass not of his commandments.

Deceive not yourselves therefore, thinking that you have faith in God, or that you love God, or do trust in him, or do fear him, when you live in sin: for then your ungodly and sinful life declareth the contrary, whatsoever ye say or think. It pertaineth to a Christian man to have this true Christian faith, and to try himself whether he hath it or no, and to know what belongeth to it, and how it doth work in him. It is not the world that we can trust to; the world, and all that is therein, is but vanity. It is God that must be our defence and protection against all temptation of wickedness and sin, errors, superstition, idolatry and all evil. If all the world were on our side, and God against us, what could the world avail us? Therefore let us set our whole faith and trust in God, and neither the world, the devil, nor all the power of them shall prevail against us. Let us therefore, good Christian people, try and examine our faith, what it is: let us not flatter ourselves, but look upon our works, and so judge of our faith what it is. Christ himself speaketh of this matter, and saith, 'The tree is known by the fruit.' Therefore let us do good works, and thereby declare our faith to be the lively Christian faith. Let us, by such virtues as ought to spring out of faith, show our election to be sure and stable, as St. Peter teacheth, 'Endeavour yourselves to make your calling and election certain by good works.' And also he saith, 'Minister or declare in your faith virtue, in virtue knowledge, in knowledge temperance, in temperance patience, again in patience godliness, in godliness brotherly charity, in brotherly charity love.' So shall we show indeed that we have the very lively Christian faith, and may so both certify our conscience the better that we be in the right faith, and also by these means confirm other men.

If these fruits do not follow, we do but mock with God, deceive ourselves, and also other men. Well may we bear the name of Christian men, but we do lack the true faith that doth belong thereunto: for true faith doth ever bring forth good works, as St. James saith: 'Show me thy faith by thy deeds.' Thy deeds and works must be an open testimonial of thy faith: otherwise thy faith, being without good works, is but the devil's faith, the faith of the wicked, a phantasy of faith, and not a true Christian faith. And like as the devils and evil people be nothing the better for their counterfeit faith, but it is unto them the more cause of damnation: so they that be christened, and have received knowledge of God, and of Christ's merits, and yet of a set purpose do live idly, without good works, thinking the name of a naked faith to be either sufficient for them, or else setting their minds upon vain pleasures of this world, do live in sin without repentance, not uttering the fruits that do belong to such an high profession; upon such presumptuous persons, and wilful sinners, must needs remain the great vengeance of God, and eternal punishment in hell, prepared for the devil and wicked livers.

Therefore as you profess the name of Christ, good Christian people, let no such phantasy and imagination of faith at any time beguile you; but be sure of your faith, try it by your living, look upon the fruits that cometh of it, mark the increase of love and charity by it toward God and your neighbour, and so shall you perceive it to be a true lively faith. If you feel and perceive such a faith in you, rejoice in it; and be diligent to maintain it, and keep it still in you; let it be daily increasing, and more and more be well working, and so shall you be sure that you shall please God by this faith; and at the length, as other faithful men have done before, so shall ye, when his will is, come to him, and receive 'the end and final reward of your faith', as St. Peter nameth it, 'the salvation of your souls': the which God grant us, that hath promised the same unto his faithful; to whom be all honour and glory, world without end. Amen.

The third of Cranmer's homilies pushes the point home with a firm attack, grounded in biblical and ancient Christian sources, on the religious practice of the English Church before King Henry VIII. It goes further than the occasional passages of invective already encountered in the homilies on salvation and faith, by aiming squarely at Roman Catholic observance; as Diarmaid MacCulloch observes, here 'for the first time Cranmer's prose became openly polemical'.[5] Parts of this piece are therefore uncomfortable to modern ears; but it offers a fascinating survey of the Archbishop's sense of the pace and necessity of the change in which he was now a prime mover and arranger.

A Homily of Good Works annexed unto Faith

In the last sermon was declared unto you, what the lively and true faith of a Christian man is; that it causeth not a man to be idle, but to be occupied in bringing forth good works, as occasion serveth.

Now, by God's grace, shall be declared the second thing that before was noted of faith; that without it can no good work be done, acceptable and pleasant unto God; 'for as a branch cannot bear fruit of itself', saith our saviour Christ, 'except it abide in the vine; so cannot you, except you abide in me. I am the vine, and you be the branches: he that abideth in me, and I in him, he bringeth forth much fruit: for without me you can do nothing.' And St. Paul proveth, that Enoch had faith, because he pleased God: 'for without faith', saith he, 'it is not possible to please God'. And again, to the Romans he saith, 'Whatsoever work is done without faith, it is sin.' Faith giveth life to the soul; and they be as much dead to God that lack faith, as they be to the world whose bodies lack souls. Without faith, all that is done of us is but dead before God, although the work seem never so gay and glorious before man. Even as a picture graven or painted is but a dead representation of the thing itself, and is without life, or any manner of moving; so be the works of all unfaithful persons before God: they do appear to be lively works, and indeed they be but dead, not availing to the eternal life: they be but shadows and shows of lively and good things, and not good and lively things indeed: for true faith doth give life to the work, and out of such faith come good works, that be very good indeed; and without it no work is good before God.

---

5 Diarmaid MacCulloch, *Thomas Cranmer* (New Haven and London: Yale University Press, 1996), p. 373.

... Now to proceed to [that which] in the former sermon was noted of faith, that is to say, what manner of works they be which spring out of true faith, and lead faithful men unto eternal life: this cannot be known so well as by our saviour Christ himself, who was asked of a certain great man the same question: 'What works shall I do', said a prince, 'to come to everlasting life?' To whom Jesus answered, 'If thou wilt come to eternal life, keep the commandments.' But the prince, not satisfied herewith, asked farther, 'Which commandments?' The scribes and Pharisees had made so many of their own laws and traditions, to bring men to heaven, besides God's commandments, that this man was in doubt whether he should come to heaven by those laws and traditions, or by the laws of God; and therefore he asked Christ, which commandments he meant. Whereunto Christ made him a plain answer, rehearsing the commandments of God, saying, 'Thou shalt not kill, Thou shalt not commit adultery, Thou shalt not steal, Thou shalt not bear false witness, Honour thy father and mother, and Love thy nighbour as thyself.' By which words Christ declared, that the laws of God be the very way that do lead to eternal life, and not the traditions and laws of men. So that this is to be taken for a most true lesson taught by Christ's own mouth, that the works of the moral commandments of God be the very true works of faith, which lead to the blessed life to come.

There follows a description of the fall of humanity, and of the consequent descent into idolatry and division, from Adam and Eve onwards, including the idol worship of the Old Testament, the pagan worship of the Romans, and an account of Jesus' dealings with the Jewish sects and groups of his time. Then Cranmer returns to a wholeheartedly Reformation strain, unleashing his full passion, now unbridled by the fear of a disapproving monarch, on the material culture of the Christianity of his youth and early adulthood. This passage is perhaps not among the easiest of Cranmer's works for a modern reader, but must rank as one of his most effective pieces of polemical prose and a remarkable insight into the convictions which evolved under Henry VIII and were then the basis for his great achievements under Edward VI, and therefore for his great legacy to the Church.

Thus have you heard how much the world, from the beginning until Christ's time, was ever ready to fall from the commandments of God, and to seek other means to honour and serve him, after a devotion imagined of their own heads; and how they extolled their own traditions as high or above God's commandments; which hath happened also in our times (the more it is to be lamented) no less than it did among the Jews, and that by the corruption, or at the least by the negligence of them that chiefly ought to have preferred God's commandments, and to have preserved the sincere and heavenly doctrine left by Christ. What man, having any judgement or learning, joined with a true zeal unto God, doth not see and lament to have entered into Christ's religion, such false doctrine, superstition, idolatry, hypocrisy and other enormities and abuses, so as by little and little, through the sour leaven thereof, the sweet bread of God's holy word hath been much hindered and laid apart? Never had the Jews in their most blindness so many pilgrimages unto images, nor used so much kneeling, kissing and censing of them, as hath been used in our time. Sects and feigned religions were neither the forty part so many among the Jews, nor more superstitiously and ungodly abused, than of late days they have been among us: which sects and religions had so many hypocritical works in their state of religion, as they arrogantly named it, that their lamps, as they said, ran always over, able to satisfy not only for their own sins, but also for all other their benefactors, brothers, and sisters of their religion, as most ungodly and craftily they had persuaded the multitude of ignorant people; keeping in divers places, as it were, marts or markets of merits, being full of their holy relics, images, shrines, and works of supererogation[6] ready to be sold. And all things which they had were called holy, holy cowls, holy girdles, holy pardoned beads, holy shoes, holy rules, and all full of holiness. And what thing can be more foolish, more superstitious, or ungodly, than that men, women, and children, should wear a friar's coat to deliver them from agues or pestilence? Or when they die, or when they be buried, cause it to be cast upon them, in hope thereby to be saved? Which superstition, although (thanks be to God) it hath been little used in this realm, yet in divers other realms it hath been and yet is used among many, both learned and unlearned.

Cranmer turns the fire of his preaching now to the monastic life in particular, and criticizes the effects of the three vows of the religious life.

---

6 This refers to the works of the saints, done above and beyond those strictly required by God. In late medieval Catholicism, these works of the saints, the 'treasury of merits' could be applied to the remission of the sins of others, usually those in purgatory. It became a key Reformation argument, and a central piece of Luther's critique of the papacy and Catholic thought.

The vow of obedience, he says, actually encouraged disobedience, by encouraging a higher loyalty to the Pope than to the monarch; the non-observance of the vow of chastity he passes over, merely alluding to the great number of scandals surrounding the religious; the vow of poverty was denied by the fabulous wealth of the monasteries, compounded by a frequent lack of charity. Then, he turns to England.

> Honour be to God, who did put light in the heart of his faithful and true minister of most famous memory, King Henry the eight, and gave him the knowledge of his word, and an earnest affection to seek his glory, and to put away all such supersititious and pharisaical sects by Antichrist invented, and set up again the true word of God, and glory of his most blessed name, as he gave the like spirit unto the most noble and famous princes, Josaphat, Josiah, and Ezechias. God grant all us the King's Highness faithful and true subjects, to feed of the sweet and savoury bread of God's own word, and (as Christ commanded) to eschew all our pharisaical and papistical leaven of man's feigned religion: which, although it were before God most abominable, and contrary to God's commandments and Christ's pure religion, yet it was extolled to be a most godly life, and highest state of perfection: as though a man might be more godly and more perfect, by keeping the rules, traditions, and professions of men, than by keeping the holy commandments of God.

After a final attack on a multitude of other abuses and pre-Reformation offences, which resulted in 'much error, superstition, idolatry, vain religion, preposterous judgement, great contention, with all ungodly living', Cranmer draws to a conclusion:

> Wherefore, as you have any zeal to the right and pure honouring of God, as you have any regard to your own souls, and to the life that is to come, which is both without pain and without end, apply yourselves chiefly above all thing to read and to hear God's word, mark diligently therein what his will is you should do, and with all your endeavour apply yourselves to follow the same. First, you must have an assured faith in God, and give yourselves wholly unto him, love him in prosperity and adversity, and dread to offend him evermore: then, for his sake, love all men, friends and foes, because they be his creation and image, and redeemed by Christ, as ye are. Cast in your minds, how you may do good unto all men unto your powers, and hurt no man. Obey all your superiors and governors; serve your

masters faithfully and diligently, as well in their absence as in their presence, not for dread of punishment only, but for conscience sake, knowing that you are bound so to do by God's commandments. Disobey not your fathers and mothers, but honour them, help them, and please them to your power. Oppress not, kill not, beat not, neither slander nor hate any man; but love all men, speak well of all men, help and succour every man as you may, yes even your enemies that hate you, that speak evil of you, and that do hurt you. Take no man's goods, nor covet your neighbour's good wrongfully; but content yourselves with that which ye get truly; and also bestow your own goods charitably, as need and case requireth. Flee all idolatry, witchcraft, and perjury; commit no manner of adultery, fornication, nor other unchasteness, in will nor in deed, with any other man's wife, widow, maid, or otherwise. And travailing continually during your life thus in the observing the commandments of God (wherein consisteth the pure, principal and direct honour of God, and which God hath ordained to be the right trade and pathway unto heaven), you shall not fail, as Christ hath promised, to come to that blessed and eternal life, where you shall live in glory and joy with God for ever: to whom be laud, honour and impery,[7] for ever and ever. Amen.[8]

The Catechism of 1548

The English translation of the Latin catechism of Justus Jonas, issued in 1548, was intended to be a helpful tool in the instruction of England's children in the form of Christianity now favoured by the Council. Its firm language against the use of images echoes that of the homilies and underscores that this was a major emphasis of Cranmer and the authorities in the early months of the new King's reign. The book was subsequently more notorious, and a stumbling-block for the Archbishop, because of its firmly Lutheran eucharistic theology, which swiftly became outdated in the liturgical change of the Edwardian Reformation. Cranmer's enemies later successfully used it against him as evidence of inconsistency. The book was probably produced in a rather hurried manner, and evidence of Cranmer's own involvement in it is rather

---

7 An archaic word, sometimes spelled Empery, for sovereignty or supreme authority.

8 Cranmer, *Remains*, vol. 2, pp. 164–77.

scant. For all that, this, the only purely Lutheran work to be published in the English Reformation, was prefaced with an elegant letter of dedication to the boy king from his 'humble subject and chaplain', and setting forth the catechism's purpose of inculcating right religion in England's children.[9]

> It is not unknown unto the whole world (most excellent prince) that your grace's father a king of most famous memory of a fervent and godly disposition and tender zeal towards the setting forth of God's glory, most diligently travailed for a true and a right reformation and a quiet concord in Christ's religion throughout all his dominions, wherein undoubtedly he brought many things to a godly purpose and effect, and did abolish and take away much blindness and ignorance of God, many great errors, fond and pernicious superstitions and abuses, that had crept into this church of England, and Ireland a long time. And I, perceiving that your majesty by the advice of your most dear uncle my Lord Protector, and the rest of your grace's most honourable council, is most desirous perfectly to finish and bring to pass, that your father did most godly begin, do think that there is nothing more necessary, for the furtherance hereof, than that it might be foreseen, how the youth and tender age of your loving subjects may be brought up and traded in the truth of God's holy word. For it is thought not to me only, but to many others, that neither your grace's father should have been enforced in his time, to have taken so great pains for the reformation of Christ's religion, neither yet your highness in this your time, should need with such great difficulty to go about to further God's cause and his true service, with so many laws, injunctions and proclamations if so great negligence of the education of the youth had not been so much suffered, and the necessary points and articles of our religion and profession omitted of those whose office and bounden duty was to have most diligently instructed the youth in the same. Or if the ancient and laudable ceremony of Confirmation had continued in the old state, and been duly used of the ministers in time convenient, where an exact and straight examination was had of all such as were of full age, both of their profession that they made in baptism touching their belief and keeping of God's commandments, with a general solemn rehearsal of the said commandments and of all the articles of their faith. Surely there

---

9 See Diarmaid MucCulloch's discussion of the catechism: *Thomas Cranmer*, p. 387.

can be no greater hope of any kind of persons, other to be brought to all honest conversation of living, or to be more apt to set forth and maintain all godliness and true religion, than of such as have been from childhood nourished and fed with the sweet milk, and as it were the pap of God's holy word, and bridled and kept in awe with his holy commandments. For commonly as we are in youth brought up, so we continue in age, and savour longest of that thing that we first receive and taste of. And as a fair table finely polished, though it be never so apt to receive either pictures of writings, yet it doth neither delight any man's eyes, neither yet profit anything, except the painter take his pencil, set to his hand, and with labour and cunning replenish it with scriptures or figures as appertaineth to his science, even so the tender wits of young children, being yet naked and bare of all knowledge through the grace of God be apt to receive God's gifts, if they be applied and instructed by such school masters, as have knowledge to bring them up and lead them forwards therein. And what can be more apt to be graven or planted in the tender hearts of youth, than God's holy word? What can lead them to a righter way to God, to the obedience of their Prince and to all virtue and honesty of life, than the sincere understanding of God's word? Which alone showeth the way how to know him, to love him and to serve him. What can better keep and stay them, that they do not suddenly and lightly fall again from their faith? What can cause them more constantly to withstand the assaults of the Devil, the world and the flesh, and manfully to bear the cross of Christ, than to learn in their youth to practise the same? And verily it seemeth no new thing that the children of them that be godly, should be thus instructed in the faith and commandments of God, even from their infancy. For doth not God command his people to teach his law, unto their children and children's children? Hath not this knowledge continued from time to time, amongst them to whom God promised to be their God, and they his people?

I knowing myself as a subject greatly bounden (and much the more by reason of my vocation) to set forward the same, am persuaded that this my small travail in this behalf taken shall not a little help the sooner to bring to pass your godly purpose. For by this little treatise, not only the youth of your grace's realm, may learn to know God, and how they may most purely and sincerely honour, glorify and serve him, and may also learn their office and duty, how they ought to behave themselves, first towards God, secondly towards your Majesty, and so towards all ministers under the same, towards their fathers and mothers, and all other persons of what sort or degree soever they be: but also many of the older sort, (such as love God, and have a zeal to his honour and glory, and in their youth through negligence were brought up in ignorance) may by hearing of their children, learn in their age, that which passed them in their youth.

And as mine intent and endeavour is to profit both, and according to mine office, to bring both to the right knowledge of God, so my most earnest and humble prayer unto God continually, shall be that my good mind and desire may have good success, and take effect according to mine expectation. Which thing I assuredly hope shall come to pass, if it would please your Highness, to suffer this little book by me offered unto your Majesty to be read, taught and learned of children of your most loving subjects, in whom is great hope of all grace, godliness and virtue.[10]

A Sermon on Rebellion

In 1549, England was convulsed by a wave of sedition, an uprising whose causes were complex and various, but certainly included the grinding poverty of many and the resistance felt by some to the religious changes of the regime, not least the new Prayer Book. Cranmer led the Church's stern denunciation of the rebellion, commandeering Bishop Edmund Bonner's pulpit in St Paul's in the summer and preaching a fiery warning against the activity of the rebels. Much of the sermon consists of a point by point rebuttal of the given reasons for the rebellion; these brief excerpts, on Cranmer's understanding of the causes of the troubles and his call for national repentance, give a sense of his grief, his anger and his pastoral and personal concern that nothing should jeopardize the religious renewal now under way.

The common sorrow of this present time, dearly beloved brethren in Christ, if I should be more led thereby, than by reason and zeal to my country, would move me rather to hold my peace, than to speak. For the great evils, which we now suffer at this present time, are to be bewailed with tears and silence, rather than with words . . . [but I] know right well that our common sorrow and lamentable

---

10 Thomas Cranmer, *A Catechism set forth by Thomas Cranmer*, ed. D. G. Selwyn (Oxford: Sutton Courtenay Press, 1978), pp. i–v.

state cannot be remedied with silence, nor good counsel can be given with holding my peace. Now therefore, in this common sorrow, I know nothing that is more able to suage our griefs, and to comfort our heaviness, than is the word of God. For as the sun many times with his beams driveth away great thick and dark clouds, and stayeth great storms of winds; so doth the light of God's word stay men's minds, bringing them from trouble to quietness, from heaviness and desperation to gladness, joy, and comfort. Wherefore I most humbly beseech Almighty God to grant me by his Spirit, that out of holy scripture I may plainly set out before your eyes the principal causes of all these tumults and seditions: for if the causes be once known, it shall be the more easy to provide remedy therefore.

Now the time requireth to declare another cause of our sedition, which is the greedy desire, and, as it were, worshipping of riches, wherewith both the high and low sort being too much blinded have brought our realm to this point. And surely nothing more hath caused great and puissant armies, realms and empires to be overthrown, than hath done the insatiable covetousness of worldly goods. For hereby, as a most strong poison, whole realms many times have come to ruin, which seemed else to have endured for ever: sundry commonwealths, which before were conserved in unity, have by incurable disorder been divided and separated into many parts. This manner of vice, if it be unseemly unto any other people, to them surely that profess Christ it is utterly shameful and detestable; which above all nations should be the true esteemers and lovers of pure godly things which be eternal and immortal, and ought to seek for right judgment and estimation of things only at their own profession. For as many of us as be truly called Christians of Christ, do confess that we be redeemed by him, not through the vain and uncertain riches of this world, but through the strong and perfect obedience whereby he submitted himself unto his Father, to be obedient even unto the death of the cross. Wordly-wise men esteem worldly riches and wealth above all other things; but the wisdom of God esteemeth obedience above all other things, that is to say, that a man should submit his will to God's will, that he should not desire to use any thing in this world, no, not his own life, but as it shall please God and be to his glory . . .

[On the lukewarmness of much English religion:] The church of God, most dearly beloved brethren, ought not to be reputed and taken as a common place, whereunto men resort only to gaze and to hear, either for their solace or their pastime. But whatsoever is there declared of the word of God, that should we devoutly receive, and so earnestly print in our minds, that we should both believe it as most certain truth, and most diligently endeavour ourselves to express the same in our manners and living. If we receive and repute the gospel as a thing most true and godly, why do we not live according to the same? If we count it as fables and trifles, why do we take upon us to give such credit and authority to it? To what purpose tendeth such dissimulation and hypocrisy? If we take it for a Canterbury Tale, why do we not refuse it? Why do we not laugh it out of place, and whistle at it? Why do we with words approve it, with conscience receive and allow it, give credit unto it, repute and take it as a thing most true, wholesome and godly, and in our living clearly reject it? . . .

[On repentance:] Hitherto ye have heard of the profit and commodity of repentance: now shall ye hear what it is, and of what parts it consisteth. And to declare it plainly and grossly unto you, it is a sorrow conceived for sins committed, with hope and trust to obtain remission by Christ, with a firm and effectual purpose of amendment, and to alter all things that hath been done amiss.

I have described unto you this heavenly medicine; which if we use, God hath promised by his prophet, that 'if our sins were so red as scarlet, they shall be made as white as snow'. But God's word hath thus much prevailed among us, that in the stead of sorrow for our sin is crept in a great looseness of living without repentance: in the stead of hope and trust of remission of our sins is come in a great boldness to sin without the fear of God: instead of amendment of our lives I see daily every thing waxeth worse and worse . . . But let us repent in time without further delay. For we have enough and overmuch already provoked God's wrath and indignation against us. Wherefore let us pray and fall down and lament before the Lord our Maker; for 'he is the Lord our God, and we are the people of his pasture and the sheep of his fold. Today if we hear his voice, let us not harden our hearts, as the people did in the desert.'[11]

---

11 Thomas Cranmer, *The works of Thomas Cranmer, Archbishop of Canterbury, Martyr 1556*, 2 vols, ed. John Edmund Cox (Cambridge: Parker Society, 1844–6), vol. 1, *Writings and disputations, relative to the sacrament of the Lord's Supper*, pp. 190–201.

A Letter of Consolation

Cranmer worked hard and lobbied furiously to attract leading continental Reformers to key academic posts in England under Edward VI.
His efforts were rewarded when Martin Bucer, Paul Fagius and Peter
Martyr Vermigli eventually arrived in 1549. Unfortunately, Fagius died
within days of taking up his chair in Hebrew at Cambridge. The letter
Cranmer wrote to Bucer on the event is another tender example of his
human warmth and heartfelt sympathy on the passing of a colleague,
friend and mentor. It draws this chapter to a close as a reminder of the
sensitivity and humanity of Cranmer, and of his private friendships
and commitments, even as his official duties demanded much of him in
public life.

> Most learned Bucer, it is not now my intention to tell you how deep
> a wound of sorrow has been caused to my feelings by the death of
> our friend Fagius, lest I should seem to irritate your wound, which,
> as I suppose, has been healed by the aid of your theology, as well as
> also in some sense by the lapse of time. But rather for the present
> I have determined to communicate to you the thoughts by which I
> myself gained consolation; not that, prudent as you are, you stand
> in need of consolations which I can give (for I know the moderation
> and reasonableness of your mind), but that by frequent repetition
> and consideration in my own mind I might by some means shake off
> this grief. In the first place, my thoughts took this turn, that it was in
> accordance with our nature to sympathize, condole, and weep with
> our friend, while he was for so long a time very grievously suffering
> from that painful disease: but now after that he has been freed from
> all sufferings, and has been translated from warfare to peace, from
> troublous waves to a haven the most still, from toils to endless felic-
> ity, it would be the act of an enemy, not of a friend, to bewail his
> state. 'For the souls of the righteous are in the Lord's hand.' And the
> Psalmist saith: 'Right dear in the sight of the Lord is the death of his
> saints.' Since therefore our friend worshipped God with true piety,
> and gave his attention and labour to the extension of the study of
> learning, there is no reason why we should not hope that, by the mercy
> of the Judge, he hath obtained that eternal life which he here com-
> menced with such diligence. I could indeed wish, if so it had pleased
> God, that he might have sojourned with us for a longer period in the
> course of this life; but since it hath seemed good to our most merci-
> ful Father to call him away to a better and more learned school, we

ought to congratulate him that Paul Fagius hath been summoned to the company of Christ and St. Paul, and to the most holy college of angels, prophets, and apostles.

By these and other means I lift up my prostrate mind, and produce better hopes and thoughts. By my letter I put you in mind of these, not because they are needful for you, but rather that by these and similar consolations you may soften and assuage the grief of that excellent woman, the wife of our friend Fagius. And I earnestly beg and entreat of you to exhort her not to give herself up to sorrow.

A certain poet hath written, 'With sincerity of grief the loss of money is lamented'; and therefore that in this respect I may in some way recover her, by this messenger I send to her twenty-seven pounds of our money; which sum although as yet I have not received it from the King's treasurer for Fagius's salary, yet I expect soon to receive it. Meanwhile that in some way I might alleviate the widow's grief, I think it better to pay this money from my own resources.[12]

The official pronouncements and proclamations of these years, of course, as well as the personal projects Cranmer pursued around them which are evidenced here, were not their, or his, abiding legacy. In 1549, Cranmer's most cherished project saw the light of day, and birthed a new experience of worship for the Church in England and, subsequently, further afield. These pieces offer a sense of the background against which the Archbishop was creating and summoning into being the most remarkable liturgical project of his or any age: the *Book of Common Prayer*.

---

12 Cranmer, *Writings and disputations*, p. 427.

4

The Books of Common Prayer

We know from Cranmer's efforts at liturgical innovation and adaptation under Henry VIII, which had enjoyed varied success, as well as from the early moves of the Edwardian years, that uniformity in reformed English religion was always dear to his heart, as was the creation of a fitting vehicle for its expression. Work on a new prayer book for use throughout the realm got under way very soon after Edward became king, and proceeded apace. In 1549, the new book was issued and its universal use commanded of all churches by Whit Sunday. From March of that year, it slowly became the shared liturgical language of the kingdom. Over time, through subsequent incarnations, it created an essentially Anglican approach to worship and prayer and to the forming of Christian community. Even the Archbishop himself probably had little sense that the publication in 1549 of a new prayer book for the English would ultimately have such a global and extraordinary effect on the worshipping life of the Church universal.

The most fascinating feature of the two prayer books, the first version and its 1552 successor, is the way in which they reveal the evolution, both of the Archbishop's thought and of the regime's religious policy. Cranmer, showing admirable pastoral wisdom and sensitivity, always advocated caution in the task of weaning the English away from what he saw as ancient error, which nevertheless had rooted itself deeply in the collective imagination, and towards the purer landscape of Protestant worship. Some have criticized him for this, but the upheavals in the nation caused by the first book help to give credence to his approach. By 1552, he was ready to take the next step and, had the young king survived, would probably have refined the Prayer Book even more, and even further away from the Roman Catholic past. Most notable in this respect were the changes wrought in just three years in the rites for Holy Communion and the burial of the dead, which this chapter will seek to compare and contrast.

Above all, though, it is important in these extracts from Cranmer's greatest achievement to gain a sense of how deeply his prose has become ingrained in the English language and of how profoundly this comparatively short work has influenced discourse both within and outside the Church. We should also remember that Cranmer was not the only author of these rites and prayers: the book owes its language and form to the work of a team of the Archbishop's closest associates. Its compilation, editorship and much of the felicity of its expression, however, belongs to him alone and is rightly described as his legacy. So too, although we must remember that Cranmer drew on a very wide and fascinating range of sources old and new in its creation, the arrangement of the elements in their final order reflects his genius and flair. The collects, short corporate prayers for particular occasions or expressing specific desires, are perhaps the books' most remarkable and characteristic achievement; we shall try to be clear with them which are perfect translations and adaptations of older texts and which sublime creations of the Archbishop's own pen.

The Preface to the Prayer Book

There was never any thing by the wit of man so well devised, or so surely established, which (in continuance of time) hath not been corrupted: as (among other things) it may plainly appear by the common prayers in the Church, commonly called divine service: the first original and ground whereof, if a man would search out by the ancient fathers, he shall find that the same was not ordained, but of a good purpose, and for a great advancement of godliness: for they so ordered the matter, that all the whole Bible (or the greatest part thereof) should be read over once in the year, intending thereby, that the clergy, and specially such as were ministers of the congregation, should (by often reading and meditation of God's word) be stirred up to godliness themselves, and be more able also to exhort other by wholesome doctrine, and to confute them that were adversaries to the truth. And further, that the people (by daily hearing of holy scripture read in the Church) should continually profit more and more in the knowledge of God, and be the more inflamed with the love of his true religion. But these many years past this godly and decent order of the ancient fathers, hath been so altered, broken and neglected, by planting in uncertain stories, legends, responses, verses, vain repetitions, commemorations and synodals, that commonly when any book of the Bible was begun: before three or four chapters were read out, all the rest were unread . . . And moreover, whereas St. Paul would have such

language spoken to the people in the Church, as they might understand and have profit by hearing the same: the service in this Church
of England (these many years) hath been read in Latin to the people,
which they understood not, so that they have heard with their ears
only: and their hearts, spirit and mind, have not been edified thereby.

. . . These inconveniences therefore considered: here is set forth such
an order, whereby the same shall be redressed. And for a readiness
in this matter, here is drawn out a Calendar for that purpose, which
is plain and easy to be understood, wherein (so much as may be) the
reading of holy scripture is so set forth, that all things shall be done
in order, without breaking one piece thereof from another . . . So that
here you have an order for prayer (as touching the reading of holy
scripture) much agreeable to the mind and purpose of the old fathers,
and a great deal more profitable and commodious, than that which
of late was used. It is more profitable, because here are left out many
things, whereof some be untrue, some uncertain, some vain and superstitious: and is ordained nothing to be read, but the very pure word of
God, the holy scriptures, or that which is evidently grounded upon the
same: and that in such a language and order, as is most easy and plain
for the understanding, both of the readers and hearers. It is also more
commodious, both for the shortness thereof, and for the plainness of
the order, and for that the rules be few and easy. Furthermore by this
order, the curates shall need none other books for their public service,
but this book and the Bible: by the means whereof, the people shall not
be at so great charge for the books, as in time past they have been.

And where heretofore, there hath been great diversity in saying and
singing in churches within this realm . . . now from henceforth all the
whole realm shall have one use. And if any would judge this way more
painful, because that all things must be read upon the book, whereas
before by the reason of so often repetition, they could say many things by
heart: if those men will weigh their labour, with the profit in knowledge,
which daily they shall obtain by reading upon the book, they will not refuse the pain, in consideration of the great profit that shall ensue thereof.

Of Ceremonies, why some be abolished and some retained

This short treatise appeared at the end of the 1549 book and at the beginning of the 1552 version, a firm but eloquent short statement of the
'middle way' approach eventually to define global Anglicanism.

Of such ceremonies as be used in the church, and have had their beginning by the institution of man: some at the first were of godly intent and purpose devised, and yet at length turned to vanity and superstition: some entered into the church by undiscreet devotion, and such a zeal as was without knowledge: and for because they were winked at in the beginning, they grew daily to more and more abuses: which not only for their unprofitableness, but also because they have much blinded the people, and obscured the glory of God, are worthy to be cut away and clean rejected. Other there be, which although they have been devised by man: yet it is thought good to reserve them still, as well for a decent order in the church (for the which they were first devised) as because they pertain to edification: whereunto all things done in the church (as the Apostle teacheth) ought to be referred. And although the keeping or omitting of a ceremony (in itself considered) is but a small thing: yet the wilfull and contemptuous transgression and breaking of a common order and discipline, is no small offence before God.

And whereas in this our time, the minds of men are so diverse, that some think it a great matter of conscience to depart from a piece of the least of their ceremonies (they be so addicted to their old customs:) and again on the other side, some be so new-fangled, that they would innovate all thing, and so do despise the old, that nothing can like them, but that is new: it was thought expedient, not so much to have respect how to please and satisfy either of these parties, as how to please God, and profit them both. And yet lest any man should be offended (whom good reason might satisfy) here be certain causes rendered, why some of the accustomed ceremonies be put away, and some retained and kept still.

Some are put away, because the great excess and multitude of them, hath so increased in these latter days, that the burden of them was intolerable, where of St. Augustine in his time complained, that they were grown to such a number, that the state of Christian people was in worse case (concerning that matter) than were the Jews.[1] And he counselled that such yolk and burden should be taken away, as time would serve quietly to do it.

---

1 This is an uncomfortable sentence to include, showing Augustine's casual and careless stereotyping of Jewish religious observance, shared to a degree by Cranmer, whose language about the Jews generally reflects the prejudices of his time but in much less graphic and condemnatory tones than others: for instance, Martin Luther. See also note on the third collect at Good Friday and 'Afterlife', below.

But what would St. Augustine have said, if he had seen the ceremonies of late days used among us? Whereunto the multitude used in his time, was not to be compared. This our excessive multitude of ceremonies was so great, and many of them so dark, that they did more confound, and darken, than declare and set forth Christ's benefits unto us.

And besides this, Christ's Gospel is not a ceremonial law (as much of Moses' law was) but it is a religion to serve God, not in bondage of the figure or shadow, but in the freedom of the spirit, being content only with those ceremonies, which do serve to a decent order and godly discipline, and such as be apt to stir up the dull mind of man, to the remembrance of his duty to God, by some notable and special signification, whereby he might be edified.

Furthermore, the most weighty cause of the abolishment of certain ceremonies was, that they were so far abused, partly by the superstitious blindness of the rude and unlearned, and partly by the unsatiable avarice of such as sought more their own lucre, than the glory of God: that the abuses could not be well taken away, the thing remaining still. But now as concerning those persons, which peradventure will be offended, for that some of the old ceremonies are retained still: if they consider that without some ceremonies, it is not possible to keep any order, or quiet discipline in the church: they shall easily perceive just cause to reform their judgements. And if they think much, that any of the old do remain, and would rather have all devised and new: Then such men granting some ceremonies convenient to be had, surely where the old may be well used, there they cannot reasonably reprove old, only for their age, without bewraying of their own folly. For in such a case, they ought rather to have reverence unto them for their antiquity, if they will declare themselves to be studious of unity and concord, than of innovations and new-fangledness, which (as much as may be with the true setting forth of Christ's religion) is always to be eschewed. Furthermore, such shall have no just cause with the ceremonies reserved, to be offended. For as those be taken away, which were most abused, and did burden men's consciences without any cause: so the other that remain, are retained for a discipline and order, which (upon just causes) may be altered and changed, and therefore are not to be esteemed equal with God's law. And moreover, they be neither dark nor dumb ceremonies: but are so set forth, that every man may understand what they do mean, and to what use they do serve. So that it is not like that they, in time to come, should be abused as

86

the other have been. And in these our doings, we condemn no other nations, nor prescribe any thing, but to our own people only. For we think it convenient that every country should use such ceremonies, as they shall think best to the setting-forth of God's honour or glory, and to the reducing of the people to a most perfect and godly living, without error or superstition. And that they should put away other things, which from time to time they perceive to be most abused, as in men's ordinances it often chanceth diversely in diverse countries.

The Order for Morning and Evening Prayer

These two short services, perhaps more than any other, have come to represent the Anglican liturgical tradition and genius that were Cranmer's greatest creation. The 1549 book, envisaging a very small (or even non-existent) congregation, employed the singular 'I' and 'my' in the prayers; by 1552, the version reproduced here, the services were extended and enriched, with plural, 'we' language, clear instructions for the daily observance of the services including the tolling of the church bell to summon a congregation, and an expectation that Matins and Evensong (renamed simply Morning and Evening Prayer in 1552) were to be major expressions of corporate worship. It is likely that the earlier expectation that Communion would be a universal weekly observance for all in the parish had already been proved unrealistic, and the services for Morning and Evening Prayer were therefore refashioned and given fresh emphasis in 1552 to become the major expression of English prayer.[2] Rubrics here are centred and in smaller print, as in the original; my annotations are in square brackets.

An order for Morning Prayer

[The service beings with selections from Scripture, after which the priest says:]

Dearly beloved brethren, the scripture moveth us in sundry places, to acknowledge and confess our manifold sins and wickedness, and that

---

2 Diarmaid MacCulloch, *Thomas Cranmer* (New Haven and London: Yale University Press, 1996), p. 510.

we should not dissemble nor cloak them before the face of Almighty God our heavenly Father, but confess them with an humble, lowly, penitent, and obedient heart, to the end that we may obtain forgiveness of the same by his infinite goodness and mercy. And although we ought at all times, humbly to acknowledge our sins before God: yet ought we most chiefly so to do, when we assemble and meet together, to render thanks for the great benefits, that we have received at his hands, to set forth his most worthy praise, to hear his most holy word, and to ask those things, which be requisite and necessary, as well for the body as the soul. Wherefore I pray and beseech you, as many as are here present, to accompany me with a pure heart and humble voice, unto the throne of the heavenly grace, saying after me:

A general confession, to be said of the whole congregation after the minister, kneeling:

Almighty and most merciful Father, we have erred and strayed from thy ways like lost sheep. We have followed too much the devices and desires of our own hearts. We have offended against thy holy laws. We have left undone those things which we ought to have done, and we have done those things which we ought not to have done: and there is no health in us: but thou, O Lord, have mercy upon us miserable offenders. Spare thou them O God, which confess their faults. Restore thou them that be penitent, according to thy promises declared unto mankind in Christ Jesu our Lord. And grant, O most merciful Father, for his sake, that we may hereafter live a godly, righteous, and sober life, to the glory of thy holy name. Amen.

The absolution to be pronounced by the minister alone:

Almighty God, the father of our Lord Jesus Christ, which desireth not the death of a sinner, but rather that he may turn from his wickedness and live: and hath given power and commandment to his ministers, to declare and pronounce to his people being penitent, the absolution and remission of their sins: he pardoneth and absolveth all them, which truly repent, and unfeignedly believe his holy Gospel. Wherefore we beseech him to grant us true repentance, and his holy spirit, that those things may please him, which we do at this present, and that the rest of our life hereafter, may be pure and holy: so that at the last, we may come to his eternal joy, through Jesus Christ our Lord.

The people shall answer: Amen.
[After the Lord's Prayer, the priest says:]

O Lord open thou our lips.

Answer: And our mouth shall show forth thy praise.

Priest: O God make speed to save us.

Answer: O Lord make haste to help us.

Priest: Glory be to the Father, and to the son: and to the holy ghost. As it was in the beginning, is now, and ever shall be: world without end. Amen.

Praise ye the Lord.

[The service lays out a series of Psalms to be said: 95, followed by those for the day, and then the lessons for the day, followed by the *Te Deum*, *Benedicite* and finally either the *Benedictus* from Luke 1 or Psalm 100. After this, the Creed is said by all, leading into the prayers, beginning with the Lord's Prayer and culminating in the responses and collects as follows.]

The Minister standing up shall say:

O Lord show thy mercy upon us.

Answer: And grant us thy salvation.

Priest: O Lord save the King.

Answer: And mercifully hear us when we call upon thee.

Priest: Endue thy ministers with righteousness.

Answer: And make thy chosen people joyful.

Priest: O Lord save thy people.

Answer: And bless thy inheritance.

Priest: Give peace in our time, O Lord.

Answer: Because there is none other that fighteth for us, but only thou O God.

Priest: O God make clean our hearts within us.

Answer: And take not thy holy spirit from us.

Then shall follow three Collects. The first of the day, which shall be the same
that is appointed at the Communion. The second for Peace. The third for
Grace to live well. And the two last Collects shall never later, but daily be
said at Morning prayer, throughout all the year as followeth.

O God, which art author of peace, and lover of concord, in knowledge of whom standeth our eternal life, whose service is perfect
freedom, defend us thy humble servants, in all assaults of our enemies, that we surely trusting in thy defence, may not fear the power
of any adversaries: through the might of Jesus Christ our Lord.
Amen.

O Lord our heavenly father, almighty and everlasting God, which
hast safely brought us to the beginning of this day: defend us in the
same with thy mighty power, and grant that this day we fall into no
sin, neither run into any kind of danger: but that all our doings may
be ordered by thy governance, to do always that is righteous in thy
sight: through Jesus Christ our Lord. Amen.

An Order for Evening Prayer

The Evening Prayer order follows a similar pattern, beginning with responses, which lead into the Psalms and Old Testament lesson, and
then *Magnificat*, followed by a New Testament lesson. The *Nunc Dimittis* follows, Simeon's achingly beautiful song from Luke's Gospel, and
leads into the Creed, and the same prayers, as for the morning. It is
perhaps the final collects which most characterize this exquisite piece of
liturgy: after that for the day, a prayer for peace (remodelled with perfect judgement from a recent English translation of an eighth-century
Latin original)[3] and a prayer for protection in the night.

The second Collect at Evening Prayer

O God, from whom all holy desires, all good counsels, and all just
works do proceed: give unto thy servants that peace which the world
cannot give: that both our hearts may be set to obey thy commandments, and also that by thee, we being defended from the fear of our

---

3 For a detailed examination of Cranmer's craftsmanship, see MacCulloch,
Thomas Cranmer, pp. 418–19.

enemies, may pass our time in rest and quietness, through the merits of Jesus Christ our Saviour. Amen.

The third Collect for aid against all perils

Lighten our darkness, we beseech thee, O Lord, and by thy great mercy, defend us from all perils and dangers of this night, for the love of thy only Son our Saviour Jesus Christ. Amen.

The Ministration of Baptism to be used in the Church

The orders for baptism do not reflect the major shift in theological emphasis seen in other rites, but do show some signs of simplification and 'cleansing' of Catholic elements: the anointing with oil is removed; the exorcism of the baby is excised; the use of the baptismal gown called the Chrisom is no longer required; and making the sign of the cross seems rather less prominent. These two versions also reveal something of Cranmer's indebtedness to a range of sources: the first prayer, about Noah and Moses, is a Lutheran invention, which remains in pared-down form in 1552. In 1549, Cranmer included elements from a seventh-century Spanish form of worship called the Mozarabic liturgy, to accompany the changing of the font water; in 1552, some of this liturgy was incorporated into the pre-baptismal prayer. Both versions indicate the desire of the Church's leaders for a reduction in private baptism and the renewal of regular public baptism, 'when the most number of people may come together, as well for that the congregation there present may testify the receiving of them that be newly baptized into the number of Christ's Church, as also because in the Baptism of infants, every man present may be put in remembrance of his own profession made unto God in his Baptism'.

[After the introductory sentences, the priest prays:]

Almighty and everlasting God, which of thy great mercy didst save Noah and his family in the Ark from perishing by water: and also didst safely lead the children of Israel, thy people through the Red Sea: figuring thereby thy holy Baptism, and by the Baptism of thy wellbeloved son Jesus Christ, didst sanctify the flood Jordan, and all other waters, to the mystical washing away of sin: We beseech thee for thy infinite mercies, that thou wilt mercifully look upon these children, sanctify them and wash them with thy holy ghost, that they, being delivered from thy wrath, may be received into the Ark of Christ's Church, and being steadfast in faith, joyful through hope, and rooted in charity, may so pass the waves of this troublesome world, that finally they may come to the land of everlasting life, there to reign with thee world without end, through Jesus Christ our Lord. Amen.

Almighty and immortal God, the aid of all that need, the helper of all that flee to thee for succour, the life of them that believe, and the resurrection of the dead: We call upon thee for these infants, that they coming to thy holy Baptism, may receive remission of their sins by spiritual regeneration. Receive them (O Lord) as thou hast promised by thy wellbeloved son, saying: Ask and you shall have, seek and you shall find, knock and it shall be opened unto you: so give now unto us that ask. Let us that seek find. Open the gate unto us that knock, that these infants may enjoy the everlasting benediction of thy heavenly washing, and may come to the eternal Kingdom, which thou hast promised by Christ our Lord. Amen.

[After a Scripture reading and invitation to baptism, the priest addresses the godparents, outlining their responsibility to speak for the children. After the examination of faith, the priest prepares for baptism, using part of the 1549 rite for the changing of the water, drawn from the Mozarabic liturgy of early medieval Spain:]

O merciful God, grant that the old Adam in these children may be so buried, that the new man may be raised up in them. Amen.

Grant that all carnal affections may die in them, and that all things belonging to the spirit, may live and grow in them. Amen.

Grant that they may have power and strength to have victory and to triumph against the devil, the world and the flesh. Amen.

Grant that whosoever is here dedicated to thee by our office and ministry, may also be endued with heavenly virtues, and everlastingly rewarded through thy mercy, O blessed lord God, who dost live and govern all things world without end. Amen.

[The baptism proceeds, after which the priest says:]

Seeing now, dearly beloved brethren, that these children be regenerate and grafted into the body of Christ's congregation: let us give thanks unto God for these benefits, and with one accord make our prayers unto almighty God that they may lead the rest of their life, according to this beginning.

Then shall be said:

Our Father which art in heaven, etc.

Then shall the Priest say:

We yield thee hearty thanks, most merciful Father, that it hath pleased thee to regenerate this infant with thy holy spirit, to receive him for thy own child by adoption, and to incorporate him into thy holy congregation. And humbly we beseech thee to grant that he, being dead unto sin, and living unto righteousness, and being buried with Christ in his death, may crucify the old man, and utterly abolish the whole body of sin: that as he is made partaker of the death of thy son, so he may be partaker of his resurrection: so that finally, with the residue of thy holy congregation, he may be inheritor of thine everlasting kingdom: through Christ our Lord. Amen.

At the last end, the Priest calling the Godfathers and Godmothers together, shall say this short exhortation following:

For as much as these children have promised by you to forsake the Devil and all his works, to believe in God, and to serve him: you must remember that it is your parts and duties to see that these infants be taught so soon as they shall be able to learn, what a solemn vow, promise, and profession they have made by you. And that they may know these things the better, ye shall call upon them to hear sermons: And chiefly ye shall provide that they may learn the Creed, the Lord's Prayer, and the ten Commandments in the English tongue, and all other things which a Christian man ought to know and believe, to his soul's health: and that these children may be virtuously brought up, to lead a godly and a Christian life, remembering always that Baptism doth represent unto us our profession, which is to follow the example of our saviour Christ, and to be made like unto him: that as he died and rose again for us, so should we which are baptised, die from sin, and rise again unto righteousness, continually mortifying all our evil and corrupt affections, and daily proceeding in all virtue, and godliness of living.

The Communion

The order for Communion underwent a significant shift in structure and theological orientation between the two prayer books of 1549 and 1552. If the earlier version was always intended as a stop-gap, offering crumbs of comfort to conservatives while uniting the realm in a single vernacular service with evangelical tones, the second version was unequivocally and unapologetically Reformed, rejecting even a Lutheran sense that the bread and wine were anything more than bread and wine, and ridding the liturgy, both of words retained in the 1549 version (altar, Mass) and of many of the ceremonies and priestly attire that went with them. By 1552, the priest stood at a plain table set longwise down the empty chancel, and presided over a memorial meal of Christ's passion and death. The service's closing instructions at a devastating stroke firmly defined what remained after the Communion service on the table – bread and wine:

> And to take away the superstition, which any person hath, or might have in the bread and wine, it shall suffice that the bread be such, as is usual to be eaten at the Table, with other meats, but the best and purest wheat bread, that conveniently may be gotten. And if any of the bread or wine remain, the Curate shall have it to his own use.

An infamous 'Black Rubric' (so called because the late timing of its insertion prevented the use of the red ink customary for rubrics), inserted against Cranmer's wishes but expressing his theology, defended the prescribed practice of kneeling to receive Communion as an act of gratitude and humility and not as an adoration 'unto any real or essential presence there being of Christ's natural flesh and blood'. Zurich had come to Canterbury: and London and Winchester and every town and city in England. The medieval Catholic past, and its intense focus on the sacrifice of the Mass, had been swept utterly away.

For all that, elements remained in common between the two versions of the service. What follows is designed to illustrate the evolution of Cranmer's liturgical intentions within these three critical years: first, a comparative table of the structure of the Communion service; then, language from the 1549 version omitted in 1552 but worthy of our memory; and, finally, an edited version of the Communion service as it existed in England at Edward's death, a fascinating reminder of a time when the Church of England found itself in step with the thoroughgoing reformed Protestant theology of Europe.

The Service in 1549

Instructions (including language of the 'Mass' and the 'altar')
Collect (unaltered in 1552)
Kyrie and *Gloria*, in English
Collect for the day and for the King (unaltered in 1552)
Readings from the Bible
The Creed
Sermon or Homily, followed by exhortation to Communion (approved text provided)
Invitation to receive Communion the following week and instructions for preparation
Offertory with biblical sentences
Preface, including the Proper Preface
Prayers for the Kingdom, the Church, the saints and the dead, including consecration of elements (the priest is instructed to make the sign of the cross, but forbidden to elevate the elements)
Lord's Prayer
Invitation to receive Communion
General confession and absolution with 'comfortable words'
Prayer of humble access ('We do not presume . . .')
Distribution of Communion, with Scripture quotations, using these phrases:

'The body of our Lord Jesus Christ which was given for thee, preserve thy body and soul unto everlasting life.
'The blood of our Lord Jesus Christ which was shed for thee, preserve thy body and soul unto everlasting life.'

Post-communion prayer
The Benediction and dismissal

The Service in 1552

Opening Instructions ('Table' is now substituted for 'Altar')
Collect
The Ten Commandments
Collect for the day and for the King
Readings from the Bible
The Creed
Sermon or Homily, followed by exhortation to remember the poor, and Scripture sentences

Offertory
Prayers for the Kingdom and the Church (all mention of the saints
and the departed gone)
Occasional Exhortation to Communion, 'when the Curate shall see
the people negligent to come to the holy Communion'
Optional call to the examination of conscience
Second Exhortation and Invitation to Communion
General confession and absolution with 'comfortable words'
Preface and Proper Preface
Prayer of Humble Access (slightly distanced now from the actual
reception)
Words of Institution, without consecration or the sign of the cross
Distribution of Communion, with these phrases:

> 'Take and eat this, in remembrance that Christ died for thee, and
> feed on him in thy heart by faith, with thanksgiving.
> 'Drink this in remembrance that Christ's blood was shed for thee,
> and be thankful.'

The Lord's Prayer
Post-communion prayer
Gloria, Benediction and Dismissal

The Supper of the Lord, and the Holy Communion, commonly called the Mass (1549)

(Sections omitted from the 1552 Prayer Book)

These two sections represent the way in which the language of the 1552
book shifted away from traditional emphases on the saints, the life of
the dead, and the 'real presence' of Christ in the Communion. There
were also, as seen in the outlines above, major shifts in structure and
especially in the content of the exhortations to receive Communion.

From the prayer 'for the whole state of Christ's church', leading into
the consecration:

> And here we do give unto thee most high praise, and hearty thanks
> for the wonderful grace and virtue, declared in all thy saints, from
> the beginning of the world: And chiefly in the glorious and most
> blessed virgin Mary, mother of thy son Jesus Christ our Lord and
> God, and in thy holy Patriarchs, Prophets, Apostles and Martyrs,

whose examples (O Lord) and steadfastness in thy faith, and keeping thy holy commandments: grant us to follow. We commend unto thy mercy (O Lord) all other thy servants, which are departed hence from us, with the sign of faith, and now do rest in the sleep of peace: Grant unto them, we beseech thee, thy mercy, and everlasting peace, and that at the day of thy general resurrection, we and all they which be of the mystical body of thy son, may altogether be set on his right hand and hear that his most joyful voice: Come unto me, O ye that be blessed of my father, and possess the kingdom, which is prepared for you, from the beginning of the world: Grant this, O father, for Jesus Christ's sake, our only mediator and advocate.

O God heavenly Father, which of thy tender mercy didst give thine only son Jesus Christ, to suffer death upon the cross for our redemption, who made there (by his one oblation once offered) a full, perfect and sufficient sacrifice, oblation and satisfaction, for the sins of the whole world, and did institute, and in his holy Gospel command us, to celebrate a perpetual memory of that his precious death, until his coming again: hear us (O merciful father) we beseech thee: and with thy holy spirit and word, vouchsafe to bl+ess and sanc+tify[4] these thy gifts, and the creatures of bread and wine, that they may be unto us the body and blood of thy most dearly beloved son Jesus Christ. Who in the same night . . .

Between the consecration and the confession:

Christ our Paschal Lamb is offered up for us, once for all, when he bare our sins on his body upon the cross, for he is the very lamb of God, that taketh away the sins of the world: wherefore let us keep a joyful and holy feast with the Lord.

The Order for the Administration of the Lord's Supper or Holy Communion (1552)

Opening collect

Almighty God, unto whom all hearts be open, all desires known, and from whom no secrets are hid: cleanse the thoughts of our hearts by

---

4 The inserted '+' indicates that the sign of the cross is made here over the elements.

the inspiration of thy holy spirit, that we may perfectly love thee, and worthily magnify thy holy name: through Christ our Lord. Amen.

From the first Exhortation

We be come together at this time, dearly beloved brethren, to feed at the Lord's supper, unto the which in God's behalf I bid you all that be here present, and beseech you for the lord Jesus Christ's sake, that ye will not refuse to come thereto, being so lovingly called and bidden of God himself. Ye know how grievous and unkind a thing it is, when a man hath prepared a rich feast, decked his table with all kind of provision, so that there lacketh nothing but the guests to sit down: and yet they which be called, without any cause most unthankfully refuse to come. Which of you in such a case would not be moved? Who would not think a great injury and wrong done unto him? . . . I for my part am here present, and according to mine office, I bid you in the name of God, I call you in Christ's behalf, I exhort you, as you love your own salvation, that ye will be partakers of this holy communion . . . It is said unto all, 'Take ye and eat; take and drink ye all of this, do this in remembrance of me.' With what face then, or with what countenance shall ye hear these words? What will this be else but a neglecting, a despising, and mocking of the Testament of Christ? Wherefore, rather than you should so do, depart you hence and give place to them that be godly disposed. But when you depart, I beseech you, ponder with yourselves from whom you depart: ye depart from the Lord's table, ye depart from your brethren, and from the banquet of most heavenly food. These things if ye earnestly consider, ye shall by God's grace return to a better mind, for the obtaining whereof, we shall make our humble petitions while we shall receive the holy communion.

Invitation to Communion

You that do truly and earnestly repent you of your sins, and be in love and charity with your neighbours, and intend to lead a new life, following the commandments of God, and walking from henceforth in his holy ways: Draw near, and take this holy Sacrament to your comfort: make your humble confession to almighty God, before this congregation here gathered together in his holy name, meekly kneeling upon your knees.

General Confession

Almighty God, father of our Lord Jesus Christ, maker of all things, Judge of all men, we acknowledge and bewail our manifold sins and wickedness, which we from time to time most grievously have committed, by thought, word and deed, against thy divine Majesty: provoking most justly thy wrath and indignation against us: we do earnestly repent, and be heartily sorry for these our misdoings: the remembrance of them is grievous unto us, the burden of them is intolerable: have mercy upon us, have mercy upon us most merciful father, for thy son our Lord Jesus Christ's sake: forgive us all that is past, and grant that we may ever hereafter serve and please thee, in newness of life, to the honour and glory of thy name: Through Jesus Christ our Lord. Amen.

Absolution by the Priest:

Almighty God our heavenly father, who of his great mercy, hath promised forgiveness of sins to all them, which with hearty repentance and true faith turn to him: have mercy upon you, pardon and deliver you from all your sins, confirm and strengthen you in all goodness, and bring you to everlasting life: through Jesus Christ our Lord. Amen.

Prayers before Communion

Lift up your hearts.

Answer: We lift them up unto the Lord.

Let us give thanks unto our Lord God.

Answer: It is meet and right so to do.

It is very meet, right, and our bounden duty, that we should at all times, and in all places, give thanks unto thee, O lord holy father, almighty everlasting God.

[A Proper Preface may follow, according to the season, including the following:]

Upon Easter Day, and seven days after:
But chiefly are we bound to praise thee, for the glorious resurrection of thy son Jesus Christ our Lord, for he is the very Paschal lamb, which was offered for us, and hath taken away the sin of the world, who by his death hath destroyed death, and by his rising to life again hath restored to us everlasting life.

Upon the Ascension Day, and seven days after:
Through thy most dear, beloved son, Jesus Christ our Lord, who after his most glorious resurrection manifestly appeared to all his Apostles, and in their sight ascended up into heaven, to prepare a place for us, that where he is, thither might we also ascend, and reign with him in glory.

Upon Whit Sunday, and six days after:
Through Jesus Christ our Lord, according to whose most true promise, the holy ghost came down this day from heaven, with a sudden great sound, as it had been a mighty wind, in the likeness of fiery tongues, lighting upon the Apostles, to teach them, and to lead them into all truth, giving them both the gift of diverse languages, and also boldness with fervent zeal, constantly to preach the Gospel unto all nations, whereby we are brought out of darkness and error, into the clear light and true knowledge of thee, and of thy son Jesus Christ.

Therefore with Angels, and Archangels, and with all the company of heaven, we laud and magnify thy glorious name, evermore praising thee and saying: Holy, holy, holy, Lord God of hosts: heaven and earth are full of thy glory: glory be to thee, O lord, most high.

The Prayer of Humble Access

We do not presume to come to this thy table (O merciful Lord) trusting in our own righteousness, but in thy manifold and great mercies: we be not worthy so much as to gather up the crumbs under thy Table, but thou art the same Lord, whose property is always to have mercy: grant us therefore (gracious Lord) so to eat the flesh of thy dear son Jesus Christ, and to drink his blood, that our sinful bodies may be made clean by his body, and our souls washed through his most precious blood, and that we may evermore dwell in him, and he in us. Amen.

Then the priest standing up shall say, as followeth:[5]

Almighty God our heavenly father, which of thy tender mercy didst give thine only son Jesus Christ, to suffer death upon the cross for our redemption, who made there (by his oblation of himself once offered) a full, perfect and sufficient sacrifice, oblation, and satisfaction,

---

5 Although this prayer opens as it did in 1549, the consecration is now removed and the prayer combined with the words of Institution.

for the sins of the whole world, and did institute, and in his holy Gospel command us to continue, a perpetual memory of that his precious death, until his coming again: Hear us O merciful father we beseech thee; and grant that we, receiving these thy creatures of bread and wine, according to thy son our saviour Jesus Christ's holy institution, in remembrance of his death and passion, may be partakers of his most blessed body and blood: who, in the same night that he was betrayed, took bread, and when he had given thanks, he brake it, and gave it to his Disciples, saying: Take, eat, this is my body which is given for you. Do this in remembrance of me. Likewise after supper he took the cup, and when he had given thanks, he gave it to them, saying: Drink ye all of this, for this is my blood of the new Testament, which is shed for you and for many, for the forgiveness of sins: do this as often as ye shall drink it in remembrance of me.

Prayer after communion

O Lord and heavenly father, we thy humble servants entirely desire thy fatherly goodness, mercifully to accept this our Sacrifice of praise and thanksgiving: most humbly beseeching thee to grant, that by thy merits and death of thy son Jesus Christ, and through faith in his blood, we and all thy whole church may obtain remission of our sins, and all other benefits of his Passion. And here we offer and present unto thee, O lord, ourselves, our souls, and bodies, to be a reasonable, holy, and lively Sacrifice unto thee: humbly beseeching thee, that all we which be partakers of this holy Communion, may be fulfilled with thy grace and heavenly benediction. And although we be unworthy, through our manifold sins to offer unto thee any sacrifice: yet we beseech thee to accept this our bounden duty and service, not weighing our merits, but pardoning our offences, through Jesus Christ our Lord; by whom and with whom, in the unity of the holy ghost, all honour and glory be unto thee, O father almighty, world without end. Amen.

Or:

Almighty and everliving God, we most heartily thank thee, for that thou dost vouchsafe to feed us, which have duly received these holy mysteries, with the spiritual food of the most precious body and blood of thy son our saviour Jesus Christ, and dost assure us thereby of thy favour and goodness toward us, and that we be very members incorporate in thy mystical body, which is the blessed company of all faithful people, and be also heirs, through hope, of thy everlasting kingdom, by the merits of the most precious death and Passion of thy dear son. We now most humbly beseech thee, O heavenly father, so to assist us with thy grace, that we may continue in that holy fellowship, and do all such good works, as thou hast prepared for us to walk in: through Jesus Christ our Lord, to whom with thee and the holy ghost, be all honour and glory, world without end. Amen.

The Blessing

The peace of God which passeth all understanding, keep your hearts and minds, in the knowledge and love of God, and of his son Jesus Christ our Lord: and the blessing of God almighty, the father, the son, and the holy ghost, be amongst you, and remain with you always. Amen.

Six Collects, 'to be said after the Offertory, when there is no Communion' (or at Morning and Evening Prayer)

Assist us mercifully, O Lord, in these our supplications and prayers, and dispose the way of thy servants, toward the attainment of everlasting salvation: that among all the changes and chances of this mortal life they may ever be defended by thy most gracious and ready help: through Christ our Lord. Amen.

O almighty Lord and everliving God, vouchsafe we beseech thee, to direct, sanctify, and govern, both our hearts and bodies, in the ways of thy laws, and in the works of thy commandments: that through thy most mighty protection, both here and ever, we may be preserved in body and soul: through our Lord and saviour Jesus Christ. Amen.

Grant we beseech thee almighty God, that the words which we have heard this day, with our outward ears, may through thy grace, be so grafted inwardly in our hearts, that they may bring forth in us the fruit of good living, to the honour and praise of thy name: through Jesus Christ our Lord. Amen.

Prevent us, O lord, in all our doings, with thy most gracious favour, and further us with thy continual help, that in all our works begun, continued and ended in thee: we may glorify thy holy name, and finally by thy mercy obtain everlasting life: through Jesus Christ our Lord. Amen.

Almighty God, the fountain of all wisdom, which knowest our necessities before we ask, and our ignorance in asking: we beseech thee to have compassion upon our infirmities, and those things which for our unworthiness we dare not, and for our blindness we cannot ask, vouchsafe to give us for the worthiness of thy son Jesus Christ our lord. Amen.

Almighty God, which hast promised to hear the petitions of them that ask in thy son's name: we beseech thee mercifully to incline thine ears to us that have made now our prayers and supplications unto thee: and grant that those things which we have faithfully asked according to thy will may effectually be obtained, to the relief of our necessity, and to the setting forth of thy glory, through Jesus Christ our Lord. Amen.

The Solemnization of Matrimony

Here, perhaps, we come to Cranmer's most abiding and perfect achievement: an act of worship whose language is exquisite, whose expression is perfectly judged, and whose influence has been incalculable. The first married Archbishop of Canterbury here gives articulation, we may assume, to some of his own most precious insights and sources of comfort, and defines for generations and centuries to come the purpose of marriage and the proper declarations and promises which should mark its inception.

The Priest shall thus say:

Dearly beloved friends, we are gathered together here in the sight of God, and in the face of this congregation, to join together this man and this woman in holy matrimony, which is an honourable estate instituted of God in Paradise, in the time of man's innocency: signifying unto us the mystical union that is betwixt Christ and his Church: which holy estate Christ adorned and beautified with his presence and first miracle that he wrought in Cana of Galilee, and is commended of Saint Paul to be honourable among all men, and is therefore not to be enterprized, nor taken in hand unadvisedly, lightly, or wantonly, to satisfy men's carnal lusts and appetites, like brute beasts that have no understanding: but reverently, discreetly, advisedly, soberly, and in the fear of God: duly considering the causes for which Matrimony was ordained. One was the procreation of children, to be brought up in the fear and nurture of the lord, and praise of God. Secondly, it was ordained for a remedy against sin, and to avoid fornication, that such persons as have not the gift of continency might marry and keep themselves undefiled members of Christ's body. Thirdly, for the mutual society, help and comfort, that the one ought to have of the other, both in prosperity and adversity, into the which holy estate these two persons present come now to be joined. Therefore, if any man can show any just cause, why they may not lawfully be joined together: let him now speak, or else hereafter for ever hold his peace.

[After a further admonition to the couple, the vows are administered to each person as follows:]

N, wilt thou have this woman/man to be thy wedded wife/husband, to live together, after God's ordinance, in the holy estate of Matrimony?

[To the man:] Wilt thou love her, comfort her, honour, and keep her, in sickness and in health? And forsaking all other, keep thee only to her as long as you both shall live?

[To the woman:] Wilt thou obey him and serve him, love, honour and keep him, in sickness and in health, and forsaking all other . . .

. . . And so either [shall] give their troth to the other. The man first saying:

I, N, take thee, N, to my wedded wife, to have and to hold from this day forward, for better, for worse, for richer, for poorer, in sickness and in health, to love and to cherish, till death us depart, according to God's holy ordinance. And thereto I plight thee my troth.

. . . and the woman taking again the man by the right hand shall say:

I, N, take thee, N, to my wedded husband, to have and to hold from this day forward, for better, for worse, for richer, for poorer, in sickness and in health, to love, cherish and to obey, till death us depart, according to God's holy ordinance. And thereto I plight thee my troth.

. . . And the man shall give unto the woman a ring . . . and shall say:

With this ring I thee wed: with my body I thee worship: and with all my wordly goods I thee endow. In the name of the Father, and of the son, and of the holy ghost. Amen.

[Priest:] Let us pray. Eternal God, creator and preserver of all mankind, giver of all spiritual grace, the author of everlasting life: Send thy blessing upon these thy servants, this man and this woman, whom we bless in thy name, that as Isaac and Rebecca lived faithfully together so these persons may surely perform and keep the vow and covenant betwixt them made: whereof this ring given and received is a token and pledge, and may ever remain in perfect love and peace together, and live according to thy laws: through Jesus Christ our Lord. Amen.

Then shall the priest join their right hands together and say:

Those whom God hath joined together, let no man put asunder.

Then shall the Minister speak unto the people:

Forasmuch as N. and N. have consented together in holy wedlock, and have witnessed the same before God and this company, and thereto have given and pledged their troth either to other, and have declared the same by giving and receiving of a ring, and by joining of hands: I pronounce that they be man and wife together . . .

God the Father, God the son, and God the holy ghost bless, preserve and keep you: the Lord mercifully with his favour look upon you, and so fill you with all spiritual benediction and grace, that you may so live together in this life, that in the world to come you may have life everlasting. Amen.

[As the congregation moves towards Communion, Cranmer includes here biblical verses about marriage and a rather charming prayer for the marriage to produce children, to be omitted in the case of those marrying later in life, and a final blessing before the sacrament:]

O merciful God and heavenly Father, by whose gracious gift mankind is increased: we beseech thee assist with thy blessing these two persons, that they may both be fruitful in procreation of children, and also live together so long in godly love and honesty, that they may see their children's children, unto the third and fourth generation, unto thy praise and honour: through Jesus Christ our Lord. Amen.

Almighty God, which at the beginning did create our first parents Adam and Eve, and did sanctify and join them together in marriage: pour upon you the riches of his grace, sanctify and bless you, that ye may please him both in body and soul, and live together in holy love, unto your lives' end. Amen.

The Order for the Burial of the Dead

Here, again, the changes between the 1549 and 1552 versions of the Prayer Book starkly illustrate the shifts in official theology which had taken place, and the 'cleaned-up' reformed liturgy of 1552 abolishes at a stroke any connection to those elements of the former Catholic service which might smack of suspicion of 'superstition'. Eamon Duffy eloquently describes how by 1552 the most obvious absentee from the service was the corpse itself, in the sense that the priest addressed himself entirely to those still living.[6] Every opportunity for those present to ponder the ongoing life of the deceased, the old practice of prayer to the saints or the doctrine of purgatory was strictly removed. Thus, in 1549, the priest, casting earth on the body, addressed the deceased directly:

I commend thy soul to God the father almighty, and thy body to the ground . . .

By 1552, as will be seen, the earth is thrown 'by some standing by', while the priest talks directly to the mourners.

The newer service also emphasized more strongly the doctrine of predestination which underlay Cranmer's mature thought of the early 1550s, as it did all the continental Reformers from Luther onwards. In 1549, while all reference to purgatory had gone, the thought and sense of the burial prayers much more reflected a future hope in the general resurrection of the dead and not a confidence in the certainty of divine election, despite the use of the language of the 'elect':

We commend into thy hands of mercy (most merciful father) the soul of this our brother departed, N. And his body we commit to the earth, beseeching thine infinite goodness, to give us grace to live in thy fear and love, and to die in thy favour: that when the judgement

---

6 Eamon Duffy, *The Stripping of the Altars* (New Haven and London: Yale University Press, 1992), pp. 474–5.

shall come which thou hast committed to thy wellbeloved son, both this our brother, and we may be found acceptable in thy sight, and receive that blessing, which thy wellbeloved son shall then pronounce to all that love and fear thee, saying: 'Come ye blessed children of my father: Receive the kingdom prepared for you before the beginning of the world, Grant this merciful father for the honour of Jesus Christ our only saviour, mediator, and advocate. Amen.

Almighty God, we give thee hearty thanks for this thy servant, whom thou hast delivered from the miseries of this wretched world, from the body of death and all temptation. And, as we trust, hast brought his soul which he committed into thy holy hands, into sure consolation and rest: Grant we beseech thee, that at the day of judgement his soul and all the souls of thy elect, departed out of this life, may with us and we with them, fully receive thy promises, and be made perfect altogether through the glorious resurrection of thy son Jesus Christ our Lord.

By 1552, the priest articulated a faith in the immediate passage of souls to heaven and a hope that this particular soul would find a place among 'the number of the elect', according to God's inscrutable wisdom. What remains in this service, however, is some of the most beautiful prose in the English language, whose composition and compilation resulted in a service whose comfort has been experienced by generations of the bereaved across multiple Christian denominations, and indeed by concert-goers of all faiths and none, hearing it set to music by many composers. The complete 1552 service is reproduced here.

The Priest meeting the corpse at the church stile, shall say: Or else the priests and clerks shall sing, and so go either unto the church, or towards the grave.

I am the Resurrection and the Life (saith the Lord): he that believeth in me, yea though he were dead, yet shall he live. And whosoever liveth and believeth in me: shall not die for ever. (John 11)

I know that my Redeemer liveth, and that I shall rise out of the earth in the last day, and shall be covered again with my skin, and shall see God in my flesh: yea, and I myself shall behold him, not with other, but with these same eyes. (Job 19)

We brought nothing into this world, neither may we carry anything out of this world. The Lord giveth, and the Lord taketh away.

Even as it pleaseth the Lord, so cometh things to pass: blessed be the name of the Lord. (I Timothy 6; Job 1)

When they come at the grave, whilst the corpse is made ready to be laid into the earth, the Priest shall say, or the priest and clerks shall sing:

Man that is born of woman hath but a short time to live, and is full of misery: he cometh up and is cut down like a flower, he flieth as it were a shadow, and never continueth in one stay. (Job 19)

In the midst of life we be in death: of whom may we seek for succour but of thee, O Lord, which for our sins justly art displeased: yet O Lord God most holy, O Lord most mighty, O holy and most merciful saviour, deliver us not into the bitter pains of eternal death. Thou knowest Lord the secrets of our hearts, shut not up thy merciful eyes to our prayers: But spare us Lord most holy, O God most mighty, O holy and merciful saviour, thou most worthy judge eternal, suffer us not at our last hour for any pains of death, to fall from thee.

Then while the earth shall be cast upon the body, by some standing by, the priest shall say:

Forasmuch as it hath pleased almighty God of his great mercy to take unto himself the soul of our dear brother here departed, we therefore commit his body to the ground, earth to earth, ashes to ashes, dust to dust, in sure and certain hope of the resurrection to eternal life, through our lord Jesus Christ: who shall change our vile body that it may be like to his glorious body, according to the mighty working whereby he is able to subdue all things to himself.

Then shall be said or sung:

I heard a voice from heaven, saying unto me: Write from henceforth, blessed are the dead which die in the lord. Even so saith the spirit, that they rest from their labours. (Rev. 14)

Then shall follow the lesson, taken out of the XV Chapter to the Corinthians, the first epistle
. . .
The lesson ended, the priest shall say:

Lord have mercy upon us.
Christ have mercy upon us.
Lord have mercy upon us.
Our father which art in heaven, etc.

Almighty God, with whom do live the spirits of them that depart hence in the lord, and in whom the souls of them that be elected, after they be delivered from the burden of the flesh, be in joy and felicity: We give thee hearty thanks, for that it hath pleased thee to deliver this, N, our brother out of the miseries of this sinful world: beseeching thee that it may please thee of thy gracious goodness, shortly to accomplish the number of thine elect, and to haste thy kingdom, that we with this our brother, and all other departed in the true faith of thy holy name, may have our perfect consummation and bliss, both in body and soul, in thy eternal and everlasting glory. Amen.

O Merciful God, the father of our Lord Jesus Christ, who is the resurrection and the life, in whom whosoever believeth shall live even though he die. And whosoever liveth and believeth in him, shall not die eternally, who also taught us (by his holy Apostle Paul) not to be sorry, as men without hope, for them that sleep in him: we meekly beseech thee (O Father) to raise us from the death of sin, unto the life of righteousness, that when we shall depart this life, we may rest in him, as our hope is this our brother doth, and that at the general resurrection in the last day, we may be found acceptable in thy sight, and receive that blessing which thy wellbeloved son shall then pronounce, to all that love and fear thee, saying: Come, ye blessed children of my father, receive the kingdom prepared for you, from the beginning of the world. Grant this we beseech thee O merciful father, through Jesus Christ our mediator and redeemer. Amen.

The Collects

These short, communal prayers with ancient roots perhaps constitute Anglicanism's greatest gift to Protestant liturgy. Cranmer, as we have seen, drew on a wide range of sources in compiling his prayers, including the Sacramentaries of the fourth-century popes Leo I and Gelasius, and their seventh-century successor, Gregory the Great. Twenty-four of them, reproduced below, are his own original composition. Of particular note are those for the saints, now including only biblical figures and drastically pared down in number and content from those with which medieval Catholics would have been familiar. As is seen in this collection, for instance, in the prayer for the feast of the Annunciation, Cranmer ensured that the focus of the petition was on the life of the believer and their relationship with the divine, almost even at the expense of the saint themselves, whose own achievements faded into the background except as illustrative virtues to which the contemporary Christian might aspire. Cranmer carefully draws scriptural lessons for the congregation from these heroes of faith, turning the force of the prayer away from the saint and towards the life of the worshipper; he strips them of any 'superstitious' elements, and very deliberately widens that for St Peter's Day to include 'all bishops and pastors', thus steering the congregation away from any past connection between Peter and the See of Rome. The remainder of these collects have been described as 'close translations of the terse Latin originals'[7] and are almost always richer in translation than they had been in the original. A selection of those appears here too, surely some of the most perfectly crafted prayers for public worship ever composed and a striking example of the translator's art exceeding that of the first writers.

Original Compositions

The First Sunday in Advent

Almighty God, give us grace, that we may cast away the works of darkness, and put upon us the armour of light, now in the time of this mortal life (in which thy son Jesus Christ came to us with great humility) that in the last day, when he shall come again in his glorious majesty, to judge both the quick and the dead: we may rise to the life immortal, through him, who liveth and reigneth with thee and the holy ghost, now and ever.

The Second Sunday in Advent

Blessed Lord, which hath caused all holy scriptures to be written for our learning: grant us that we may in such wise hear them, read, mark, learn, and inwardly digest them: that by patience and comfort of thy holy word, we may embrace and ever hold fast the blessed hope of everlasting life, which thou hast given us in our saviour Jesus Christ.

---

7 M. R. Dudley, *The Collect in Anglican Liturgy* (Collegeville: Liturgical Press, 1994), pp. 6–7.

Christmas Day

Almighty God, which hast given us thy only begotten son to take our nature upon him, and this day to be born of a pure virgin: Grant that we being regenerate and made thy children by adoption and grace, may daily be renewed by thy holy spirit, through the same our lord Jesus Christ, who liveth and reigneth with thee and the holy ghost, now and ever.

The Circumcision of Christ

Almighty God, which madest thy blessed son to be circumcised and obedient to the law for man: grant us the true circumcision of the spirit, that our hearts and all our members being mortified from all worldly and carnal lusts, may in all things obey thy blessed will: through the same thy son Jesus Christ our Lord.

The Sunday called Quinquagesima[8]

O Lord which dost teach us, that all our doings without charity are nothing worth: send thy holy ghost, and pour into our hearts that most excellent gift of charity, the very bond of peace and all virtues, without the which, whosoever liveth, is counted dead before thee: Grant this for thy only son Jesus Christ's sake.

The First Day of Lent

Almighty and everlasting God, which hatest nothing which thou hast made, and dost forgive the sins of all them that be penitent: Create and make in us new and contrite hearts, that we worthily lamenting our sins, and knowledging our wretchedness, may obtain of thee, the God of all mercy, perfect remission and forgiveness, through Jesus Christ.

The First Sunday in Lent

O Lord, which for our sake, didst fast forty days and forty nights: Give us grace to use such abstinence, that our flesh being subdued to the spirit, we may ever obey thy godly monitions, in righteousness and true holiness, to thy honour and glory, which livest and reignest, etc.

---

8 The Sunday before Ash Wednesday.

Good Friday (second collect at Communion)[9]

Merciful God, who hast made all men, and hatest nothing that thou hast made, nor wouldest the death of a sinner, but rather that he should be converted and live; have mercy upon all Jews, Turks, Infidels and heretics, and take from them all ignorance, hardness of heart, and contempt of thy word: and so fetch them home, blessed Lord, to thy flock, that they may be saved among the remnant of the true Israelites, and be made one fold under one shepherd, Jesus Christ our Lord; who liveth and reigneth, etc.

Easter Sunday

Almighty God, which through thy only begotten son Jesus Christ, hast overcome death, and opened unto us the gate of everlasting life: we humbly beseech thee, that as by thy special grace, preventing us, thou dost put in our minds good desires: so by thy continual help we may bring the same to good effect, through Jesus Christ our Lord: who liveth and reigneth, etc.

The Second Sunday after Easter

Almighty God, which hast given thy holy son to be unto us, both a sacrifice for sin, and also an example of Godly life; Give us the grace that we may always most thankfully receive that his inestimable benefit, and also daily endeavour ourselves to follow the blessed steps of his most holy life.

The Sunday after the Ascension Day

O God, the king of glory, which hast exalted thine only son Jesus Christ, with great triumph unto thy kingdom in heaven: we beseech thee leave us not comfortless, but send to us thine holy ghost to

---

9 This collect is included for completeness, reflecting a Cranmerian mixture of traditional Holy Week intercessions and new language for them. In its prayers for the conversion of Jews, Muslims and 'heretics', it reflects its setting, and so causes some pain to the modern reader. It may be noted that the traditional Roman Catholic version of this prayer included the adjective 'faithless' of the Jews, which Cranmer omits, preferring to stress God's universal love for all. These prayers for the conversion of the Jewish people were omitted from the Roman Catholic liturgy only after Pope John XXIII interrupted a Good Friday liturgy to order the priest to remove the word 'faithless'; subsequently, his Second Vatican Council of the 1960s permanently deleted the phrase from the service. The Church today must still wrestle, both with its history of anti-Jewishness and with formulating a more inclusive theology for relating to those of other faiths in a globalized world.

comfort us, and exalt us unto the same place, whither our Saviour Christ is gone before: who liveth and reigneth, etc.

Saint Thomas the Apostle

Almighty everliving God, which for the more confirmation of the faith, didst suffer thy holy Apostle Thomas, to be doubtful in thy son's resurrection: grant us so perfectly, and without all doubt to believe in thy son Jesus Christ, that our faith in thy sight never be reproved: hear us, O lord, through the same Jesus Christ: to whom with thee and the holy ghost be all honour, etc.

Saint Matthias' Day

Almighty God, which in the place of the traitor Judas, didst choose thy faithful servant Matthias, to be of the number of thy twelve Apostles: Grant that thy church being always preserved from false Apostles: may be ordered and guided by faithful and true pastors: Through Jesus Christ our Lord.

The Annunciation of the Virgin Mary

We beseech thee Lord, pour thy grace into our hearts, that as we have known Christ thy son's incarnation, by the message of an Angel: so by his cross and passion: we may be brought unto the glory of his resurrection: through the same Christ our Lord.

Saint Mark's Day

Almighty God, which hast instructed thy holy Church, with the heavenly doctrine of thy Evangelist Saint Mark: give us grace so to be established by thy holy gospel, that we be not, like children, carried away with every blast of vain Doctrine: Through Jesus Christ our Lord.

Saint Philip and James

Almighty God, whom truly to know is everlasting life: Grant us perfectly to know thy son Jesus Christ, to be the way, the truth and the life, as thou hast taught Saint Philip, and other the Apostles: Through Jesus Christ our Lord.

Saint Barnabas, Apostle

Lord Almighty, which hast indued thy holy Apostle Barnabas, with singular gifts of thy holy ghost: let us not be destitute of thy manifold gifts, nor yet of grace to use them always to thy honour and glory: Through Jesus Christ our Lord.

Saint John Baptist

Almighty God, by whose providence thy servant John Baptist was wonderfully born, and sent to prepare the way of thy son our saviour by preaching of penance: make us so to follow his doctrine and holy life, that we may truly repent, according to his preaching, and after his example constantly speak the truth, boldly rebuke vice, and patiently suffer for the truth's sake: through Jesus Christ our Lord.

Saint Peter's Day

Almighty God, which by thy son Jesus Christ hast given to thy Apostle Saint Peter many excellent gifts, and commandest him earnestly to feed thy flock: make we beseech thee, all bishops and pastors diligently to preach thy holy word and the people obediently to follow the same, that they may receive the crown of everlasting glory, through Jesus Christ our Lord.

Saint James the Apostle

Grant, O merciful God, that as thine holy Apostle James, leaving his father and all that he had, without delay, was obedient unto the calling of thy son Jesus Christ, and followed him: so we, forsaking all worldly and carnal affections, may be evermore ready to follow thy commandments: through Jesus Christ our Lord.

Saint Matthew

Almighty God, which by thy blessed son didst call Matthew from the receipt of custom to be an Apostle and Evangelist: Grant us grace to forsake all covetous desires, and inordinate love of riches, and to follow thy said son Jesus Christ: who liveth and reigneth etc.

Saint Luke the Evangelist

Almighty God which called Luke the physician, whose praise is in the gospel, to be a physician of the soul: may it please thee by the wholesome medicines of his doctrine, to heal all the diseases of our souls: through thy son Jesus Christ our Lord.

Simon and Jude, Apostles

Almighty God, which hast builded thy congregation upon the foundation of the Apostles and Prophets, Jesus Christ himself being the head corner stone: grant us to be joined together in unity of spirit by their doctrine, that we may be made an holy temple acceptable to thee: through Jesus Christ our Lord.

All Saints

Almighty God, which hast knit together thy elect in one Communion and fellowship, in the mystical body of thy son Christ our Lord: grant us grace so to follow thy holy Saints in all virtues, and godly living, that we may come to those unspeakable Joys, which thou hast prepared for them that unfeignedly love thee: Through Jesus Christ our Lord.

A Selection of Collects translated by Cranmer into English

Second Sunday of Lent (Gregorian Sacramentary)

Almighty God, which dost see that we have no power of ourselves to help ourselves; keep thou us both outwardly in our bodies, and inwardly in our souls; that we may be defended from all adversities which may happen to the body, and from all evil thoughts which may assault and hurt the soul; through Jesus Christ, etc.

The Sunday next before Easter (Gelasian Sacramentary)

Almighty and everlasting God, which of thy tender love toward man, hast sent our Saviour Jesus Christ, to take upon him our flesh, and to suffer death upon the cross, that all mankind should follow the example of his great humility; mercifully grant that we both follow the example of his patience, and be made partakers of his resurrection; through the same Jesus Christ our lord.

Easter Day (Gelasian Sacramentary, alt.)

Almighty God, which through thy only begotten son Jesus Christ, hast overcome death, and opened unto us the gate of everlasting life: we humbly beseech thee, that as by thy special grace, preventing us, thou dost put in our minds good desires: so by thy continual help we may bring the same to good effect, through Jesus Christ our Lord: who liveth and reigneth, etc.

God Truly Worshipped

Whitsunday (Gregorian Sacramentary, with additions)

God, which as upon this day hast taught the hearts of thy faithful people, by sending to them the light of thy holy spirit, grant us by the same spirit to have a right judgement in all things; and evermore to rejoice in his holy comfort; through the merits of Jesus Christ our saviour; who liveth and reigneth with thee, in the unity of the same spirit, one God, world without end.

The Fourth Sunday after Trinity (Gregorian Sacramentary)

God the protector of all that trust in thee, without whom nothing is strong, nothing is holy; increase and multiply upon us thy mercy; that thou being our ruler and guide, we may so pass through things temporal, that we finally lose not the things eternal: Grant this heavenly father, for Jesus Christ's sake our Lord.

The Sixth Sunday after Trinity (Gregorian and Gelasian Sacramentaries)

God, which hast prepared to them that love thee such good things as pass all man's understanding; Pour into our hearts such love toward thee, that we loving thee in all things, may obtain thy promises, which exceed all that we can desire; through Christ our Lord.

The Twelfth Sunday after Trinity (Sacramentary of Leo)

Almighty and everlasting God, which art always more ready to hear than we to pray, and art wont to give more than either we desire or deserve; Pour down upon us the abundance of thy mercy; forgiving us those things whereof our conscience is afraid, and giving unto us that that our prayer dare not presume to ask, through Jesus Christ our Lord.

The Twenty-Fifth Sunday after Trinity (Gregorian Sacramentary)

Stir up we beseech thee, O Lord, the wills of thy faithful people, that they, plenteously bringing forth the fruit of good works, may of thee, be plenteously rewarded; through Jesus Christ our Lord.

5

'Friendship, Love, and Concord': Cranmer on the Eucharist

In the early 1550s, after a quarter of a century as a scholar in Cambridge and almost 20 years after his appointment to Canterbury, Cranmer finally published a major work of theology. To be fair, his time had been in great demand, and his achievements by 1550 were substantial. What turned him now to writing? A combination of factors seems to have been at play. First, the 'make haste slowly' approach of the early Edwardian years had brought him some criticism from those wanting him to reveal his hand as a thoroughgoing Reformer more boldly; in the *Defence*, he did so concerning one of the most central issues of the Reformation: the Eucharist. Secondly, the same halting history of his own reformation in England had left an open goal for his opponents to shoot at. The first Book of Common Prayer had contained a decidedly Lutheran, 'real presence', view of what happened at Communion: as traditionalists were thrilled to point out. The catechism of 1548, too, had been simply an English rendering of a continental Lutheran work and in some ways a real step backwards. Under fire, both from those wanting him to move more quickly and from those not wanting to move at all and resenting even those innovations already undertaken, Cranmer showed his hand. Finally, the *Defence* was clearly Cranmer's way of signalling the beginning of a new, bolder, more unashamedly reformed theology for the English Church, the opening salvo of a fresh initiative whose doctrine would be enshrined liturgically in the second Prayer Book and officially in the Forty-Two Articles.[1]

The *Defence of the True and Catholic Doctrine of the Sacrament of the Body and Blood of our Saviour Christ with a Confutation of Sundry Errors concerning the same, grounded and stablished upon God's Holy Word, and approved by the consent of the Most Ancient Doctors of the Church* did not have the catchiest title, but it did contain Cranmer's mature eucharistic theology, eloquently expressed. Published in 1550,

---

1 Diarmaid MacCulloch, *Tudor Church Militant* (London: Penguin, 1999), pp. 92–3.

it sought to silence his foes and courageously chart the pure reformed theology of the Edwardian Church. Cranmer's own shift away from believing in the real presence of Christ at the altar had happened only three years or so earlier[2] and had been somewhat hidden beneath his official liturgies, as he sought with characteristic caution to move the realm slowly in the right direction. Now, it was fully revealed, clothed in biblical mandate and the authority, as he saw it, of the Church's great theologians. The book falls into five sections: the first outlining the true doctrine of the Eucharist, the second rejecting transubstantiation, the third exploring the true nature of Christ's presence in the sacrament, the fourth dealing with issues concerning those who consume unworthily. The fifth and final section attempts to lay to rest another great Reformation controversy, by seeking to abolish the idea of the Eucharist as a sacrifice in itself and by emphasizing the Protestant insistence on the once-for-all nature of Christ's death on the cross.

A Defence

A Preface to the Reader

Our Saviour Christ Jesus according to the will of his eternal Father, when the time thereto was fully complished, taking our nature upon him, came into this world from the high throne of his Father, to declare unto miserable sinners good news; to heal them that were sick; to make the blind to see, the deaf to hear, the dumb to speak; to set prisoners at liberty; to show that the time of grace and mercy was come; to give light to them that were in darkness and the shadow of death; and to preach and give pardon and full remission of sin to all his elected. And to perform the same, he made a sacrifice and oblation of his own body upon the cross, which was a full redemption, satisfaction, and propitiation, for the sins of the whole world. And to commend this his sacrifice unto all his faithful people, and to confirm their faith and hope of eternal salvation in the same, he hath ordained a perpetual memory of his said sacrifice, daily to be used

---

2 For a fuller discussion, see Introduction, above; Diarmaid MacCulloch, *Thomas Cranmer* (New Haven and London: Yale University Press, 1996), pp. 380–92; and Peter Newman Brooks, *Thomas Cranmer's Doctrine of the Eucharist: An Essay in Historical Development* (London: Macmillan, 1992). MacCulloch disagrees with Brooks's characterization of the final phase of Cranmer's thought as 'true presence', preferring 'spiritual presence' for reasons discussed earlier.

in the Church to his perpetual laud and praise, and to our singular comfort and consolation; that is to say, the celebration of his holy supper, wherein he doth not cease to give himself with all his benefits, to all those that duly receive the same supper according to his blessed ordinance.

Cranmer goes on to outline a strong objection to one Catholic use of the Mass: the belief that Masses enabled the reduction of the time spent by the dead in purgatory, which he denounces as an implication that Christ's work was insufficient. He also takes aim at the sectarianism of medieval religion, and the fact that people used not to understand the words of the liturgy, before lauding his own achievements in public life:

> This was of late years the face of religion within this realm of England, and yet remaineth in divers realms. But, (thanks be to Almighty God and to the King's Majesty, with his father, a prince of most famous memory,) the superstitious sects of monks and friars, that were in this realm, be clean taken away; the Scripture is restored unto the proper and true understanding; the people may daily read and hear God's heavenly word, and pray in their own language which they understand, so that their hearts and mouths may go together, and be none of those people of whom Christ complained, saying, 'These people honour me with their lips, but their hearts be far from me.' Thanks be to God, many corrupt weeds be plucked up, which were wont to rot the flock of Christ, and to let the growing of the Lord's harvest.

Cranmer concludes by claiming that the two 'chief roots' of religious error in England were the doctrine of transubstantiation and the idea that the priest celebrating Mass is himself making a sacrifice for the dead. The task of the book is to uproot these tap roots of Catholic belief in England and beyond.

The First Book

The Supper of the Lord, otherwise called the Holy Communion or Sacrament of the Body and Blood of our Saviour Christ, hath been of many men, and by sundry ways, very much abused; but specially within these four or five hundred years. Of some it hath been used as a sacrifice propitiatory for sin, and otherwise superstitiously, far from the intent that Christ did first ordain the same at the beginning: doing therein great wrong and injury to his death and passion. And of other some it hath been very lightly esteemed, or rather contemned and despised, as a thing of small or none effect. And thus between both the parties hath been much variance and contention in divers places of Christendom. Therefore to the intent that this holy sacrament, or Lord's Supper, may hereafter neither of the one party be contemned or lightly esteemed, nor of the other party be abused to any purpose other than Christ himself did first appoint and ordain the same, and that so the contention of both parties may be quieted and ended; the most sure and plain way is, to cleave unto holy Scripture. Wherein whatsoever is found, must be taken for a most sure ground and an infallible truth; and whatsoever cannot be grounded upon the same (touching our faith) is man's device, changeable and uncertain.

Cranmer proceeds to lay out some key biblical texts concerning the Eucharist: and especially those from John's Gospel, the Gospel accounts of the Last Supper, and Paul's description to the church in Corinth of the institution of the Lord's Supper.

By these words of Christ rehearsed of the Evangelists, and by the doctrine also of St. Paul, (which he confesseth that he received of Christ,) two things specially are to be noted. First, that our Saviour Christ called the material bread which he brake, his body, and the wine which was the fruit of the vine, his blood.

And yet he spake not this to the intent that men should think, that material bread is his very body, or that his very body is material bread; neither that wine made of grapes is his very blood, or that his very blood is wine made of grapes; but to signify unto us (as St. Paul saith) that the cup is a communion of Christ's blood that was shed for us, and the bread is a communion of his flesh that was crucified for us. So that although, in the truth of his human nature, Christ be in heaven, and sitteth on the right hand of God the Father, yet whosoever eateth of that bread in the supper of the Lord, according to Christ's institution and ordinance, is assured of Christ's own promise and testament, that he is a member of his body, and receiveth the benefits of his passion which he suffered for us upon the cross. And likewise he that drinketh of that holy cup in that supper of the Lord, according to Christ's institution, is certified by Christ's legacy and testament, that he is made partaker of the blood of Christ which was shed for us . . . Thus is declared the sum of all that Scripture speaketh of the eating and drinking, both of the body and blood of Christ, and also of the sacrament of the same.

And as these things be most certainly true, because they be spoken by Christ himself, the author of all truth, and by his holy apostle St. Paul, as he received them of Christ, so all doctrines contrary to the same be most certainly false and untrue, and of all Christian men to be eschewed, because they be contrary to God's word. And all doctrine concerning this matter, that is more than this, which is not grounded upon God's word, is of no necessity, neither ought the people's heads to be busied, or their consciences troubled with the same. So that things spoken and done by Christ, and written by the holy Evangelists and St. Paul, ought to suffice the faith of Christian people, as touching the doctrine of the Lord's Supper, and holy communion or sacrament of his body and blood.

Which thing being well considered and weighed, shall be a just occasion to pacify and agree both parties, as well them that hitherto have contemned or lightly esteemed it, as also them which hitherto, for lack of knowledge or otherwise, ungodly abused it.

Christ ordained the sacrament to move and stir all men to friendship, love and concord, and to put away all hatred, variance, and discord, and to testify a brotherly and unfeigned love between all them that be the members of Christ; but the Devil, the enemy of Christ and of all his members, hath so craftily juggled herein, that of nothing riseth so much contention as of this holy sacrament.

God grant, that all contention set aside, both the parties may come to this holy communion with such a lively faith in Christ, and such an unfeigned love to all Christ's members, that as they carnally eat with their mouth this sacramental bread and drink the wine, so spiritually they may eat and drink the very flesh and blood of Christ, which is in heaven, and sitteth on the right hand of his Father; and that finally by his means they may enjoy with him the glory and kingdom of heaven. Amen.

Although in this treaty of the sacrament of the body and blood of our Saviour Christ, I have already sufficiently declared the institution and meaning of the same, according to the very words of the gospel and St. Paul, yet it shall not be in vain somewhat more at large to declare the same, according to the mind as well of holy Scripture as of old ancient authors; and that so sincerely and plainly, without doubts, ambiguities, or vain questions, that the very simple and unlearned people may easily understand the same, and be edified thereby.

And this by God's grace is mine only intent and desire, that the flock of Christ dispersed in this realm (among whom I am appointed a special pastor) may no longer lack the commodity and fruit which springeth of this heavenly knowledge. For the more clearly it is understood, the more sweetness, fruit, comfort and edification it bringeth to the godly receivers thereof.

He begins by describing the spiritual hungering and thirsting after God described in the Bible, and common to humanity, before coming to his point:

Whosoever hath this godly hunger is blessed of God, and shall have meat and drink enough, as Christ himself said: 'Blessed be they that hunger and thirst for righteousness, for they shall be filled full'. And on the other side, they that see not their own sinful and damnable estate, but think themselves holy enough, and in good case and condition enough, as they have no spiritual hunger, so shall they not be fed of God with any spiritual food. For as Almighty God feedeth them that be hungry, so doth he send away empty all that be not hungry.

But this hunger and thirst is not easily perceived of the carnal man: for when he heareth the Holy Ghost speak of meat and drink, his mind is by and by in the kitchen and buttery, and he thinketh upon his dishes and pots, his mouth and his belly.

But the Scripture in sundry places useth special words, whereby to draw our gross minds from the fantasying of our teeth and belly, and from this carnal and fleshly imagination. For the Apostles and disciples of Christ, when they were yet carnal, knew not what was meant by this kind of hunger and meat, and therefore, when they desired him to eat, to withdraw their minds from carnal meat, he said unto them: 'I have other meat to eat, which you know not.' And why knew they it not? Forsooth because their minds were gross as yet, and had not received the fulness of the Spirit. And therefore our Saviour Christ, minding to draw them from this grossness, told them of another kind of meat than they fantasied; as it were, rebuking them, for that they perceived not that there was any other kind of eating and drinking, besides that eating and drinking which is with the mouth and the throat.

Likewise when he said to the woman of Samaria: 'Whosoever shall drink of that water that I shall give him shall never be thirsty again': they that heard him speak those words might well perceive, that he went about to make them well acquainted with another kind of drinking, than is the drinking with the mouth and throat. For there is no such kind of drink, that with once drinking can quench the thirst of a man's body for ever. Wherefore in saying, 'He shall never be thirsty again', he did draw their minds from drinking with the mouth unto another kind of drinking whereof they knew not, and unto another kind of thirsting wherewith as yet they were not acquainted. Also when our Saviour Christ said, 'He that cometh to me shall not hunger; and he that believeth in me shall never be thirsty'; he gave them a plain watchword, that there was an other kind of meat and drink than that wherewith he fed them at the other side of the water, and another kind of hungering and thirsting than was the hungering and thirsting of the body.

Wherefore as here before in the first note is declared the hunger and drought of the soul, so it is now secondly to be noted, what is the meat, drink, and food of the soul.

The meat, drink, food and refreshing of the soul, is our Saviour Christ; as he said himself: 'Come unto me all you that travail and be laden, and I will refresh you. – And if any man be dry', saith he, 'let him come to me and drink. He that believeth in me, floods of water of life shall flow out of his belly. – And I am the bread of life', saith Christ, 'he that cometh to me shall not be hungry; and he that believeth in me shall never be dry'. For as meat and drink do comfort the hungry body, so doth the death of Christ's body, and the shedding of his blood, comfort the soul, when she is after her sort hungry. What thing is it that comforteth and nourisheth the belly? Forsooth, meat and drink. By what names then shall we call the body and blood of our Saviour Christ (which do comfort and nourish the hungry soul) but by the names of meat and drink? And this similitude caused our Saviour to say, 'My flesh is very meat, and my blood is very drink.' For there is no kind of meat that is comfortable to the soul, but only the death of Christ's blessed body; nor no kind of drink that can quench her thirst, but only the blood-shedding of our Saviour Christ, which was shed for her offences.

For as there is a carnal generation and a carnal feeding and nourishment, so is there also a spiritual generation, and a spiritual feeding.

The third thing to be noted is this, that although our Saviour Christ resembleth his flesh and blood to meat and drink, yet he far passeth and excelleth all corporal meats and drinks. For although corporal meats and drinks do nourish and continue our life here in this world, yet they begin not our life. For the beginning of our life we have from our fathers and mothers; and the meat, after we be begotten, doth feed and nourish us, and so preserve us for a time. But our Saviour Christ is both the first beginner of our spiritual life, (who first begetteth us unto God his Father), and also afterward he is our lively food and nourishment.

Fourthly, it is to be noted, that the true knowledge of these things is the true knowledge of Christ; and to teach these things is to teach Christ; and the believing and feeling of these things is the believing and feeling of Christ in our hearts. And the more clearly we see, understand, and believe these things, the more clearly we see and understand Christ, and have more fully our faith and comfort in him.

And although our carnal generation and our carnal nourishment be known to all men by daily experience and by our common senses; yet this our spiritual generation and our spiritual nutrition be so obscure and hid unto us, that we cannot attain to the true and perfect knowledge and feeling of them, but only by faith, which must be grounded upon God's most holy word and sacraments.

And for this consideration our Saviour Christ hath not only set forth these things most plainly in his holy word, that we may hear them with our ears; but he hath also ordained one visible sacrament of spiritual regeneration in water, and another visible sacrament of spiritual nourishment in bread and wine, to the intent that, as much as is possible for man, we may see Christ with our eyes, smell him at our nose, taste him with our mouths, grope him with our hands, and perceive him with all our senses. For as the word of God preached putteth Christ into our ears; so likewise these elements of water, bread and wine, joined to God's word, do after a sacramental manner put Christ into our eyes, mouths, hands, and all our senses.

And for this cause Christ ordained baptism in water, that as surely as we see, feel, and touch water with our bodies, and be washed with water; so assuredly ought we to believe, when we be baptized, that Christ is verily present with us, and that by him we be newly born again spiritually, and washed from our sins, and grafted into the stock of Christ's own body, and be apparelled, clothed and harnessed with him in such wise, that as the Devil hath no power against Christ, so hath he none against us, so long as we remain grafted in that stock, and be clothed with that apparel, and harnessed with that armour. So that the washing in water of baptism is, as it were, a showing of Christ before our eyes, and a sensible touching, feeling, and groping of him, to the confirmation of the inward faith which we have in him.

And in like manner Christ ordained the sacrament of his body and blood in bread and wine, to preach unto us, that as our bodies be fed, nourished and preserved with meat and drink, so (as touching our spiritual life towards God) we be fed, nourished, and preserved by the body and blood of our Saviour Christ; and also that he is such a preservation unto us, that neither the devils of hell, nor eternal death, nor sin, can be able to prevail against us, so long as by true and constant faith we be fed and nourished with that meat and drink. And for this cause Christ ordained this sacrament in bread and wine, (which we eat and drink, and be chief nutriments of our body,) to the intent that as surely as we see the bread and wine with our eyes, smell them with our noses, touch them with our hands, and taste them with our mouths; so assuredly ought we to believe, that Christ is our spiritual life and sustenance of our souls, like as the said bread and wine is the food and sustenance of our bodies. And no less ought we to doubt, that our souls be fed and live by Christ, than that our bodies be fed and live by meat and drink. Thus our Saviour Christ knowing us to be in this world, as it were, but babes and weaklings in faith, hath ordained sensible signs and tokens, whereby to allure and draw us to more strength and more constant faith in him. So that the eating and drinking of this sacramental bread and wine is, as it were, a showing of Christ before our eyes, a smelling of him with our noses, a feeling and groping of him with our hands, and an eating, chewing, digesting and feeding upon him to our spiritual strength and perfection.

Fifthly, it is to be noted, that although there be many kinds of meats and drinks which feed the body, yet our Saviour Christ (as many ancient authors wrote) ordained this sacrament of our spiritual feeding in bread and wine, rather than in other meats and drinks, because that bread and wine do most lively represent unto us the spiritual union and knot of all faithful people, as well unto Christ, as also amongst themselves. For like as bread is made of a great number of grains of corn, ground, baken, and so joined together that thereof is made one loaf; and an infinite number of grapes be pressed together in one vessel, and thereof is made wine; likewise is the whole multitude of true Christian spiritually joined, first to Christ, and then among themselves together, in one faith, one baptism, one holy spirit, one knot and bond of love.

Sixthly, it is to be noted, that as the bread and wine which we do eat, be turned into our flesh and blood, and be made our very flesh and very blood, and be so joined and mixed with our flesh and blood that they be made one whole body together, even so be all faithful Christians spiritually turned into the body of Christ, and be so joined unto Christ, and also together among themselves, that they do make but one mystical body of Christ, as St. Paul saith: 'We be one bread and one body, as many as be partakers of one bread and one cup.' And as one loaf is given among many men, so that every one is partaker of the same loaf, and likewise one cup of wine is distributed unto many persons, whereof every one is a partaker; even so our Saviour Christ (whose flesh and blood be represented by the mystical bread and wine in the Lord's Supper) doth give himself unto all his true members, spiritually to feed them, nourish them, and to give them continual life by him. And as the branches of a tree, or member of a body, if they be dead or cut off, neither live, nor receive any nourishment or sustenance of the body or tree; so likewise ungodly and wicked people, which be cut off from Christ's mystical body or be dead members of the same, do not spiritually feed upon Christ's body and blood, nor have any life, strength, or sustentation thereby.

Seventhly, it is to be noted, that whereas nothing in this life is more acceptable before God, or more pleasant unto man, than Christian people to live together quietly in love and peace, unity and concord: this sacrament doth most aptly and effectuously move us thereunto. For when we be made all partakers of this one table, what ought we to think, but that we be all members of one spiritual body, (whereof Christ is the head,) that we be joined together in one Christ, as a great number of grains of corn be joined together in one loaf. Surely they have very hard and stony hearts, which with these things be not moved. And more cruel and unreasonable be they than brute beasts, that cannot be persuaded to be good to their Christian brethren and neighbours, (for whom Christ suffered death,) when in this Sacrament they be put in remembrance, that the Son of God bestowed his life for his enemies. For we see by daily experience, that eating and drinking together maketh friends, and continueth friendship. Much more then ought the table of Christ to move us so to do. Wild beasts and birds be made gentle by giving them meat and drink; why then should not Christian men wax meek and gentle with this heavenly meat of Christ? Hereunto we be stirred and moved as well by the bread and wine in this holy Supper, as by the words of holy Scripture recited in the same. Wherefore whose heart soever this holy sacrament, communion, and supper of Christ, will not kindle with love unto his neighbours, and cause him to put out of his heart all envy, hatred, and malice, and to grave in the same all amity, friendship, and concord, he deceiveth himself if he think that he hath the spirit of Christ dwelling within him.

The eighth thing that is to be noted is, that this spiritual meat of Christ's body and blood, is not received in the mouth, and digested in the stomach, (as corporal meats and drinks commonly be,) but it is received with a pure heart and a sincere faith. And the true eating and drinking of the said body and blood of Christ, is with a constant and lively faith to believe, that Christ gave his body and shed his blood upon the cross for us, and that he doth so join and incorporate himself to us, that he is our head, and we his members, and flesh of his flesh, and bone of his bones, having him dwelling in us, and we in him. And herein standeth the whole effect and strength of this sacrament. And this faith God worketh inwardly in our hearts by his Holy Spirit, and confirmeth the same outwardly to our ears by hearing of his word, and to our other senses by eating and drinking of the sacramental bread and wine in his holy Supper.

What thing then can be more comfortable to us, than to eat this meat and drink this drink? Whereby Christ certifieth us, that we be spiritually and truly fed and nourished by him, and that we dwell in him and he in us. Can this be showed unto us more plainly, than when he saith himself, 'He that eateth me, shall live by me.'

From this masterly exposition of the main points of his argument, Cranmer shifts to a less charitable condemnation of his Catholic opponents' views of transubstantiation, real presence, and the daily sacrifice of the Mass. The Second Book, similarly, deals with 'The Error of Transubstantiation' and piles up biblical and ancient Christian authorities against the view that bread and wine in the Eucharist are transformed into Christ's flesh and blood. Cranmer's knowledge of the sources here is spectacular, the result of long years of scholarship; his mastery and formidable recall of them are matched by considerable skill in argument. Ambrose, Augustine, John Chrysostom, Cyprian and others are deployed against the teachings of the Roman Catholic Church, with the aim of proving the idea of transubstantiation to be a relatively new innovation, resting on either a misunderstanding or a downright perversion of scriptural wisdom and ancient teaching. Sometimes, the argument becomes technical, about finer points of ancient philosophy or figures of speech, but Cranmer is never less than fully engaged (perhaps rather vitriolically so) and compelling.

Having very negatively attacked his opponents and sought to undermine the basis of their views, Cranmer now turns in the third book more positively, to seek to teach 'the manner how Christ is present in his Supper'.

For a plain explication . . . it is not unknown to all true faithful Christian people, that our Saviour Christ, being perfect God, and in all things equal and coeternal with his Father, for our sakes became also a perfect man, taking flesh and blood of his blessed mother and Virgin Mary, and, saving sin, being in all things like unto us, adjoining unto his divinity a most perfect soul and a most perfect body; his soul being endued with life, sense, will, reason, wisdom, memory, and all other things required to the perfect soul of man; and his body being made of very flesh and bones, not only having all members of a perfect man's body in due order and proportion, but also being subject to hunger, thirst, labour, sweat, weariness, cold, heat, and all other like infirmities and passions of man, and unto death also, and that the most vile and painful upon the cross. And after his death he rose again with the selfsame visible and palpable body, and appeared therewith, and showed the same unto his Apostles, and specially to Thomas, making him to put his hands into his side and feel his wounds. And with the selfsame body he forsook this world, and ascended into heaven, (the apostles seeing and beholding his body when it ascended,) and now sitteth at the right hand of his Father, and there shall remain until the last day, when he shall come to judge the quick and the dead.

This is the true catholic faith which the Scripture teacheth, and the universal Church of Christ hath ever believed from the beginning, until within these four or five hundred years last past, that the Bishop of Rome . . . hath set up a new faith and belief of their own devising, that the same body really, corporally, naturally and sensibly is in this world still, and that in a hundred thousand places at one time, being enclosed in every pix and bread consecrated.

And although we do affirm according to God's word, that Christ is in all persons that truly believe in him, in such sort, that with his flesh and blood he doth spiritually nourish them and feed them, and giveth them everlasting life, and doth assure them thereof, as well by the promise of his word, as by the sacramental bread and wine in his holy supper, which he did institute for the same purpose, yet we do not a little vary from [these] errors.

Cranmer now proceeds to elucidate thirteen 'comparisons' between Catholic and Reformed understandings of the Communion, returning to his assertion that the credal belief in Christ's ascension denies the Catholic and affirms the Reformed approaches. His explication of the bodily ascension of Christ is further reinforced by the usual authorities in Scripture and ancient Christian authors, with a special emphasis on Augustine, but also including other less well-known sources. The argument finally comes down to one disputed verse, in the Gospel accounts of the Last Supper, in which Jesus declares of the bread, 'This is my body'. It is on the interpretation of this one phrase that the matter rests, and Cranmer is forthright and clear in his explanation. We might note the enlightened rationalism of these paragraphs, and the Archbishop's repudiation of the lively, yet mystical understanding of the preceding medieval era which now to him seems merely magical and superstitious.

> Truth it is indeed, that the words be as plain as may be spoken; but that the sense is not so plain, it is manifest to every man that weighteth substantially the circumstances of the place. For when Christ gave the bread to the disciples, and said, 'This is my body', there is no man of any discretion, that understandeth the English tongue, but he may well know by the order of the speech, that Christ spake those words of the bread, calling it his body, as all the old authors also do affirm, although some of the papists deny the same. Wherefore this sentence cannot mean as the words seem and purport, but there must needs be some figure or mystery in this speech, more than appeareth in the plain words. For by this manner of speech plainly understood without any figure as the words lie, can be gathered none other sense, but that bread is Christ's body, and that Christ's body is bread, which all Christian ears do abhor to hear. Wherefore in these words needs be sought out another sense and meaning than the words of themselves do bear.
>
> And although the true sense and understanding of these words be sufficiently declared before, when I spake of transubstantiation; yet to make the matter so plain that no scruple or doubt shall remain, here is occasion given more fully to intreat thereof. In which process shall be showed, that these sentences of Christ, 'This is my body', 'This is my blood', be figurative speeches.
>
> That bread, I say, that is one of the creatures here in earth among us, and that groweth out of the earth, and is made of many grains of corn beaten into flour, and mixed with water, and so baken and made into bread, of such sort as other our bread is, that hath neither sense nor reason, and finally, that feedeth and nourisheth our bodies; such bread Christ called his body, when he said, 'This is my body'; and such wine as is made of grapes pressed together and thereof is made drink which nourisheth the body, such wine he called his blood.

This is the true doctrine, confirmed as well by holy Scripture, as by all ancient authors of Christ's Church, both Greeks and Latins, that is to say, that when our Saviour Christ gave bread and wine to his disciples, and spake these words, 'This is my body', 'This is my blood', it was very bread and wine which he called his body and blood.

Now this being fully proved, it must needs follow consequently, that this manner of speaking is a figurative speech: for in plain and proper speech it is not true to say, that bread is Christ's body, or wine his blood. For Christ's body hath a soul, life, sense and reason: but bread hath neither soul, life, sense nor reason.

Likewise in plain speech it is not true, that we eat Christ's body, and drink his blood. For eating and drinking, in their proper and usual signification, is with the tongue, teeth and lips to swallow, divide and chew in pieces: which thing to do to the flesh and blood of Christ, is horrible to be heard of any Christian.

So that these speeches, 'To eat Christ's body and drink his blood', 'To call bread his body, or wine his blood', be speeches not taken in the proper signification of every word, but by translation of these words, 'eating', and 'drinking' from the signification of a corporal thing to signify a spiritual thing; and by calling a thing that signifieth, by the name of the thing which is signified thereby: which is no rare nor strange thing, but an usual manner and phrase in common speech.

To prove his point, Cranmer now deploys his usual sources to show, both how common figures of speech are in the Bible, and how, as he understands it, ancient Christian writers seem to have taken such use of language for granted. He makes particular use here of the fifth-century Greek theologian, Theodoret, whose dialogues were an important contribution to the disputes of his day about the person and nature of Jesus, and of the third-century Latin martyr, Cyprian. It was via Cyprian, too, that Cranmer's image, quoted above, of the many grains and grapes being pressed together to make one loaf and thus forge and signify unity had come.[3] Amid this sometimes complicated and often lengthy quotation and discussion of these ancient books, we conclude this survey of Book Three with two nuggets of pure Cranmer, one on the act of consecration which, in his view, had assumed a distorted

---

3 For more on Cranmer's use of ancient authors, see Diarmaid MacCulloch, *Thomas Cranmer*, pp. 467–8.

importance in Roman Catholic theology and practice, and then finally his summary of the thought of the eighth-century Saint John of Damascus, on how Christ is present at the Holy Communion.

Consecration is the separation of any thing from a profane and wordly use unto a spiritual and godly use.

And therefore when usual and common water is taken from other uses, and put to the use of baptism, in the name of the Father, and of the Son, and of the Holy Ghost, then it may rightly be called consecrated water, that is to say, water put to an holy use.

Even so when common bread and wine be taken and severed from other bread and wine, to the use of the holy communion, that portion of bread and wine, although it be of the same substance that the other is from the which it is severed, yet it is now called consecrated or holy bread and holy wine.

Not that the bread and wine have or can have any holiness in them, but that they be used to an holy work, and represent holy and godly things. And therefore St. Dionysne[4] calleth the bread holy bread, and the cup an holy cup, as soon as they be set upon the altar to the use of the holy communion.

But specially they may be called holy and consecrated, when they be separated to that holy use by Christ's own words, which he spake for that purpose, saying of the bread, 'This is my body'; and of the wine, 'This is my blood'.

So that commonly the authors, before those words be spoken, do take the bread and wine but as other common bread and wine; but after those words be pronounced over them, then they take them for consecrated and holy bread and wine.

Not that the bread and wine can be partakers of any holiness of godliness, or can be the very body and blood of Christ; but that they represent the very body and blood of Christ, and the holy food and nourishment which we have by him. And so they be called by the names of the body and blood of Christ, as the sign, token, and figure is called by the name of the very thing which it showeth and signifieth.

The sum of Damascene his doctrine in this matter is this. That as Christ, being both God and man, hath in him two natures; so hath

---

4 A reference to Pseudo-Dionysius the Areopagite, a late fifth- to early sixth-century theologian whose works were once attributed to a convert of St Paul in Athens from Acts 17. Cranmer is alluding to his *Ecclesiastical Hierarchy* here.

he two nativities, one eternal and the other temporal. And so likewise we, being as it were double men, or having every one of us two men in us, the new man and the old man, the spiritual man and the carnal man, have a double nativity: one of our first carnal father, Adam, by whom, as by ancient inheritance, cometh unto us malediction and everlasting damnation; and the other of our heavenly Adam, that is to say, of Christ, by whom we be made heirs of celestial benediction and everlasting glory and immortality.

And because this Adam is spiritual, therefore our generation by him must be spiritual, and our feeding must be likewise spiritual. And our spiritual generation by him is plainly set forth in baptism, and our spiritual meat and food is set forth in the holy Communion and Supper of the Lord. And because our sights be so feeble that we cannot see the spiritual water wherewith we be washed in baptism, nor the spiritual meat wherewith we be fed at the Lord's table; therefore to help our infirmities, and to make us the better to see the same with a pure faith, our Saviour Christ hath set forth the same, as it were before our eyes, by sensible signs and tokens, which we be daily used and accustomed unto.

And because the common custom of men is to wash in water, therefore our spiritual regeneration in Christ, or spiritual washing in his blood, is declared unto us in baptism by water. Likewise our spiritual nourishment and feeding in Christ, is set before our eyes by bread and wine, because they be meats and drinks which chiefly and usually we be fed withal; that as they feed the body, so doth Christ with his flesh and blood spiritually feed the soul.

And therefore the bread and wine be called examples of Christ's flesh and blood, and they be called his very flesh and blood, to signify unto us, that as they feed us carnally, so do they admonish us that Christ with his flesh and blood doth feed us spiritually and most truly unto everlasting life.

And as Almighty God by his most mighty word and his Holy Spirit and infinite power brought forth all creatures in the beginning, and ever sithence[5] hath preserved them; even so by the same word and power he worketh in us from time to time this marvellous spiritual generation and wonderful spiritual nourishment and feeding, which is wrought only by God, and is comprehended and received of us by faith.

And as bread and drink by natural nourishment be changed into a man's body, and yet the body is not changed, but the same that it was

---

5 Since then.

before; so although the bread and wine be sacramentally changed into Christ's body, yet his body is the same and in the same place that it was before, that is to say, in heaven, without any alteration of the same.

And the bread and wine be not so changed into the flesh and blood of Christ, that they be made one nature, but they remain still distinct in nature, so that the bread in itself is not his flesh, and the wine his blood, but unto them that worthily eat and drink the bread and wine to them the bread and wine be his flesh and blood; that is to say, by things natural and which they be accustomed unto, they be exalted unto things above nature. For the sacramental bread and wine be not bare and naked figures, but so pithy and effectuous, that whosoever worthily eateth them, eateth spiritually Christ's flesh and blood, and hath by them everlasting life.

Wherefore whosoever cometh to the Lord's table, must come with all humility, fear, reverence, and purity of life, as to receive not only bread and wine, but also our Saviour Christ both God and man, with all his benefits, to the relief and sustentation both of their bodies and souls.

Book Four deals with 'The Eating and Drinking of the Body and Blood of our Saviour Christ', countering the notion implied by a belief in transubstantiation that sinners could consume Christ. Here, Cranmer's predestinarian theology pokes through again, along with a more general assertion that only those who come to the table with a heart rightly disposed towards God truly gain the benefits of the sacrament. He tackles also the difficult verse from Paul's first letter to Corinth, concerning those who 'eat and drink their own damnation'. In the process, he deals sharply with the critics of the 1548 Catechism and its 'real presence' Lutheran sacramental theology, accusing these 'ignorant persons' of 'lack of understanding' and attempting, perhaps rather disingenuously, to claim that the book pointed to a different view in figurative language. The book then concludes with a final appeal to remember the centrality of such language in all discussion of the Eucharist. His argument buttressed with all the usual external authorities, Cranmer seeks to make a watertight case, summarized in the extracts below.

And every good and faithful Christian man feeleth in himself how he feedeth of Christ, eating his flesh and drinking of his blood. For he putteth the whole hope and trust of his redemption and salvation in that only sacrifice, which Christ made upon the cross, having his body there broken, and his blood there shed for the remission of his sins. And this great benefit of Christ the faithful man earnestly considereth in his mind, cheweth and digesteth it with the stomach of his heart, spiritually receiving Christ wholly into him, and giving again himself wholly unto Christ . . . For as Christ is spiritual meat, so he is spiritually eaten and digested with the spiritual part of us, and giveth us spiritual and eternal life.

It is evident and manifest, that all men, good and evil, may with their mouths visibly and sensibly eat the sacrament of Christ's body and blood; but the very body and blood themselves be not eaten but spiritually, and that of the spiritual members of Christ, which dwell in Christ, and have Christ dwelling in them, by whom they be refreshed, and have everlasting life.

Forasmuch as the bread and wine in the Lord's Supper do represent unto us the very body and blood of our Saviour Christ, by his own institution and ordinance; therefore, although he sit in heaven at his Father's right hand, yet should we come to this mystical bread and wine with faith, reverence, purity, and fear, as we would do, if we should come to see and receive Christ himself sensibly present. For unto the faithful, Christ is at his own holy table present with his mighty Spirit and grace, and is of them more fruitfully received, than if corporally they should receive him bodily present. And therefore they that shall worthily come to this God's board, must after due trial of themselves consider, first who ordained this table, also what meat and drink they shall have that come thereto, and how they ought to behave themselves thereat. He that prepared the table is Christ himself. The meat and drink wherewith he feedeth them that come thereto as they ought to do, is his own body, flesh, and blood. They that come thereto must occupy their minds in considering, how this body was broken for them, and his blood shed for their redemption. And so they ought to approach to this heavenly table with all humbleness of heart, and godliness of mind, as to the table wherein Christ himself is given. And they that come otherwise to this holy table, they come unworthily, and do not eat and drink Christ's flesh and blood, but eat and drink their own damnation; because they do not duly consider Christ's very flesh and blood, which be offered there spiritually to be eaten and drunken, but despising Christ's most holy Supper, do come thereto as it were to other common meats and drinks, without regard of the Lord's body, which is the spiritual meat of that table.

But all that love and believe Christ himself, let them not think that Christ is corporally in the bread, but let them lift up their hearts unto heaven, and worship him sitting there at the right hand of the Father. Let them worship him in themselves, whose temples they be, in whom he dwelleth and liveth spiritually: but in no wise let them worship him as being corporally in the bread; for he is not in it, neither spiritually, as he is in man; nor corporally, as he is in heaven; but only sacramentally, as a thing may be said to be in the figure, whereby it is signified.

In the fifth and final book, Cranmer turns to the nature of the sacrifice of Christ, and that of the Eucharist, denying Roman Catholic belief in the work of the priest at the altar. He relies heavily on biblical models to make his case that Christ's one death on the cross is of a vastly different character than the believer's frequent participation in Communion.

For Christ offered not the blood of calves, sheep, and goats, as the priests of the old law used to do; but he offered his own blood upon the cross. And he went not into an holy place made by man's hand, as Aaron did, but he ascended up into heaven, where his eternal Father dwelleth; and before him he maketh continual supplication for the sins of the whole world, presenting his own body, which was torn for us, and his precious blood, which of his most gracious and liberal charity he shed for us upon the cross.

And that sacrifice was of such force, that it was no need to renew it every year, as the bishops did of the old testament; whose sacrifices were many times offered, and yet were of no great effect or profit, because they were sinners themselves that offered them, and offered not their own blood, but the blood of brute beasts; but Christ's sacrifice, once offered, was sufficient for evermore.

Another kind of sacrifice there is [besides Christ's propitiatory sacrifice on the cross], which doth not reconcile us to God, but is made of them that be reconciled by Christ, to testify our duties unto God, and to show ourselves thankful unto him; and therefore they be called sacrifices of laud, praise and thanksgiving.

The first kind of sacrifice Christ offered to God for us; the second kind we ourselves offer to God by Christ.

And by the first kind of sacrifice Christ offered also us unto his Father; and by the second we offer ourselves and all that we have, unto him and his Father.

And although in the old testament there were certain sacrifices, called sacrifices for sin, yet they were no such sacrifices that could take away our sins in the sight of God; but they were ceremonies ordained to this intent, that they should be, as it were, shadows and figures, to signify beforehand the excellent sacrifice of Christ that was to come, which should be the very true and perfect sacrifice for the sins of the whole world.

And for this signification they had the name of a sacrifice propitiatory, and were called sacrifices for sins, not because they indeed took away our sins, but because they were images, shadows, and figures, whereby godly men were admonished of the true sacrifice of Christ then to come, which should truly abolish sin and everlasting death.

Wherefore all godly men, although they did use those sacrifices ordained of God, yet they did not take them as things of that value and estimation, that thereby they should be able to obtain remission of their sins before God.

But they took them partly for figures and tokens ordained of God, by the which he declared, that he would send that seed which he promised, to be the very true sacrifice for sin, and that he would receive them that trusted in that promise, and remit their sins for the sacrifice after to come.

As for like purposes we use, in the church of Christ, sacraments by him instituted . . . but the true reconciliation and forgiveness of sin before God, neither the fathers of the old law had, nor yet we have, but only by the sacrifice of Christ, made in the mount of Calvary. And the sacrifices of the old law were prognostications and figures of the same then to come, as our sacraments be figures and demonstrations of the same now passed.

Now by these foresaid things may every man easily perceive, that the offering of the priest in the mass, or the appointing of his ministration at his pleasure to them that be quick or dead, cannot merit and deserve, neither to himself, nor to them for whom he singeth or sayeth, the remission of sins . . . for if only the death of Christ be the oblation, sacrifice, and price, wherefore our sins be pardoned, then the act or ministration of the priest cannot have the same office.

If we be indeed, as we profess, Christian men, we may ascribe this honour and glory to no man, but to Christ alone. Wherefore let us give the whole laud and praise hereof unto him; let us fly only to him for succour; let us hold him fast, and hang upon him, and give ourselves wholly to him. And forasmuch as he hath given himself to death for us, to be an oblation and a sacrifice to his Father for our sins, let us give ourselves again to him, making unto him an oblation, not of goats, sheep, kine, and other beasts that have no reason, as was accustomed before Christ's coming; but of a creature that hath reason, that is to say, of ourselves, not killing our own bodies, but mortifying the beastly and unreasonable affections that would gladly rule and reign in us.

This theme brings Cranmer finally to a discussion on the nature of priesthood, and a rather important section on the Reformation idea of what Luther called 'the priesthood of all believers', with radically inclusive and almost egalitarian overtones:

As in a prince's house the officers and ministers prepare the table, and yet other, as well as they, eat the meat and drink the drink; so do the priests and ministers prepare the Lord's Supper, read the Gospel, and rehearse Christ's words; but all the people say thereunto, Amen; all remember Christ's death, all give thanks to God, all repent and offer themselves an oblation to Christ, all take him for their Lord and Saviour, and spiritually feed upon him; and in token thereof, they eat the bread and drink the wine in his mystical Supper.

The humble confession of all penitent hearts, their knowledging of Christ's benefits, their thanksgiving for the same, their faith and consolation in Christ, their humble submission and obedience to God's will and commandments, is a sacrifice of laud and praise, accepted and allowed of God no less than the sacrifice of the priest. For Almighty God, without respect of person, accepteth the oblation and sacrifice of priest and lay person, of king and subject, of master and servant, of man and woman, of young and old, yea of English, French, Scot, Greek, Latin, Jew, and Gentile; of every man according to his faithful and obedient heart unto him; and that through the sacrifice propitiatory of Jesu Christ.

But thanks be to the eternal God, the manner of the holy communion, which is now set forth within this realm, is agreeable with the institution of Christ, with St. Paul and the old primitive and apostolic Church, with the right faith of the sacrifice of Christ upon the cross for our redemption, and with the true doctrine of our salvation, justification, and remission of all our sins by that only sacrifice.

Now resteth nothing but that all faithful subjects will gladly receive and embrace the same, being sorry for their former ignorance; and every man repenting himself of his offences against God, and amending the same, may yield himself wholly to God, to serve and obey him all the days of his life, and often to come to the holy Supper, which our Lord and Saviour Christ hath prepared; and he there corporally eateth the very bread, and drinketh the very wine; so spiritually he may feed of the very flesh and blood of Jesu Christ his Saviour and Redeemer, remembering his death, thanking him for his benefits, and looking for none other sacrifice at no priest's hands for remission of his sins, but only trusting to his sacrifice, which being both the High Priest, and also the Lamb of God, prepared from the beginning to take away the sins of the world, offered up himself once for ever in a sacrifice of sweet smell unto his Father, and by the same paid the ransom for the sins of the whole world; who is before us entered into heaven, and sitteth at the right hand of his Father, as a Patron, Mediator, and Intercessor for us; and there hath prepared places for all them that be lively members of his body, to reign with him for ever, in the glory of his Father; to whom with him, and the Holy Ghost, be glory, honour, and praise, for ever and ever. Amen.[6]

An Answer

The full and future extent of the reformation now under way in England was boldly revealed in the *Defence*, and the disclosure provoked the inevitable conservative backlash. Cranmer's arch-rival and long-time opponent, Stephen Gardiner, who was Bishop of Winchester until his deprivation in 1550, lost little time in producing a treatise of his own, the *Explication and Assertion*, responding to the Archbishop's theology and claims to scholarly insight in the *Defence*. Gardiner aimed to undermine Cranmer's arguments by asserting the continuity of Christian belief in transubstantiation and the sacrifice of the Mass throughout history. The tone of Gardiner's book was polemical though learned, often dense and difficult to read, and its content and superior tone provoked a furious response from Cranmer, the *Answer . . . unto a Crafty and Sophistical Cavillation, devised by Stephen Gardiner.* The title says it all: reprinting Gardiner's own writing in bite-sized chunks, Cranmer set about trying to demolish not only their coherence and truth but also Gardiner's character and claims to learning. Cranmer indeed at the outset tried to diminish his foe, claiming that only Gardiner's former rank as a bishop warrants a reply, and that his book 'else needed

---

6 The full text of Cranmer's *Defence* is in Thomas Cranmer, *Remains of Thomas Cranmer*, 4 vols, ed. Henry Jenkins (Oxford: Oxford University Press, 1833), vol. 2, pp. 275–463.

greatly none answer for any great learning or substance of matter that is in it'.[7] Later, the theologian Cranmer says to the lawyer Gardiner, from a great height:

> For although in such weighty matters of scripture and ancient authors you must needs trust your men, (without whom I know you can do very little, being brought up from your tender age in other kinds of study), yet I, having exercised myself in the study of scripture and divinity from my youth, (whereof I give most hearty lauds and thanks to God), have learned now to go alone, and do examine, judge and write all such weighty matters myself; although, I thank God, I am neither so arrogant nor so wilful, that I will refuse the good advice, counsel, and admonition of any man, be he man or master, friend or foe.[8]

The animus between the two men, to be sure, went back far and down deep, and Gardiner had surely been central in plots under Henry to end Cranmer's career and even his life. Even so, the tone of *An Answer* is tedious and sometimes very strident, the result of a sense of outrage and anger rarely publicly witnessed at this personal level from this usually gentle soul. The *Answer* often also takes the form of merely expanded forms of arguments expressed in the *Defence*, the text of which is reprinted verbatim again within its pages, interspersed with attacks on another critic, Richard Smith, and followed by hair-splitting defences of the use of particular authors and authorities. Thus, here we select only the highlights of this book which, though dense and closely argued, hardly represents the best of Cranmer's intellect, character or style. It does, however, reflect again the new openness and ambition of Cranmer's intentions for the Church of England early in the 1550s.

> [Returning to the central question of what Christ meant when saying at the Last Supper 'This is my body':]
> Where you speak of the miraculous working of Christ, to make bread his body, you must first learn that the bread is not made really Christ's body, nor the wine his blood, but sacramentally. And the miraculous working is not in the bread, but in them that duly eat the

---

7 Thomas Cranmer, *The works of Thomas Cranmer, Archbishop of Canterbury, Martyr 1556*, 2 vols, ed. John Edmund Cox (Cambridge: Parker Society, 1844–6), vol. 1, *Writings and disputations, relative to the sacrament of the Lord's Supper*, p. 4.

8 Cranmer, *Writings and disputations*, p. 224.

bread, and drink that drink. For the marvellous work of God is in the feeding; and it is christian people that be fed, and not the bread.

And so the true confession and belief of the universal church, from the beginning, is not such as you many times affirmed, but never can prove: for the catholic church acknowledges no such division between Christ's holy flesh and his Spirit, that life is renewed in us by his holy Spirit, and increased by his holy flesh; but the true faith confesseth that both be done by his holy Spirit and flesh jointly together, as well the renovation, as the increase of our life. Wherefore you diminish here the effect of baptism, wherein is not given only Christ's Spirit, but whole Christ . . . And although Christ be not corporally in the bread and wine, yet Christ used not so many words, in the mystery of his holy supper, without effectual signification. For he is effectually present, and effectually worketh not in the bread and wine, but in the godly receivers of them, to whom he giveth his own flesh spiritually to feed upon, and his own blood to quench their great inward thirst.[9]

On the ways in which the sacrament can be treated:

Some eat only the sacrament of Christ's body, but not the very body itself; some eat his body and not the sacrament; and some eat the sacrament and the body both together. The sacrament (that is to say, the bread) is corporally eaten and chewed with the teeth in the mouth: the very body is eaten and chewed with faith in the spirit. Ungodly men, when they receive the sacrament, they chew in their mouths, like unto Judas, the sacramental bread, but they eat not the celestial bread, which is Christ. Faithful christian people, such as be Christ's true disciples, continually from time to time record in their minds the beneficial death of our Saviour Christ, chewing it by faith in the cud of their spirit, and digesting it in their hearts, feeding and comforting themselves with that heavenly meat, although they daily receive not the sacrament thereof; and so they eat Christ's body spiritually, although not the sacrament thereof. But when such men for their more comfort and consolation of eternal life, given unto them by Christ's death, come unto the Lord's holy table; then, as before they fed spiritually upon Christ, so now they feed corporally also upon the sacramental bread: by which sacramental feeding in Christ's promises, their former spiritual feeding is increased, and they grow and wax

---

9 Cranmer, *Writings and disputations*, pp. 34-5.

continually more strong in Christ, until at the last they shall come to the full measure and perfection in Christ.[10]

And, on the purpose of the Communion:

And although all christian men ought of duty continually to worship Christ being in heaven, yet because we be negligent to do our duties therein, his word and sacraments be ordained to provoke us thereunto: so that, although otherwise we forget our duties, yet when we come to think of any of his sacraments, we should be put in remembrance thereof. And therefore said Christ, as St. Paul writeth, 'As often as you shall eat this bread and drink this cup, show forth the Lord's death until he come.' And, 'Do this,' said Christ, 'in remembrance of me.' And the worshipping of Christ in his glory should be ever continual, without either 'before' or 'after'. Nevertheless, forasmuch as by reason of our infirmity, ingratitude, malice, and wickedness, we go far from our offices and duties herein, the sacraments call us home again, to do that thing which before we did omit, that at the least we may do at some time that which we should do at all times.[11]

On how bread can be also at the same time called 'the body of Christ', with a veiled accusation towards his addressee:

The bread is not so clearly delivered from the name of bread, that it is no bread at all . . . nor that it may not be called by the name of bread; but it is so delivered, that commonly it is called by the higher name of the Lord's body, which to us it representeth. As you and I were delivered from our surnames, when we were consecrated bishops, sithens which time we have so commonly been used of all men to be called bishops, you of Winchester, and I of Canterbury, that the most part of the people know not that your name of Gardiner, and mine Cranmer. And I pray God that we, being called to the name of lords, have not forgotten our own baser estates, that once we were simple squires. And yet should he have done neither of us wrong, that should have called us by our right names, no more than St. Paul doth any injury to the bread in the sacrament, calling it bread, although it also hath a higher name of dignity, to be called the body of Christ. And as the bread, being a figure of Christ's body, hath the

---

10 Cranmer, *Writings and disputations*, pp. 70–1.
11 Cranmer, *Writings and disputations*, p. 235.

name thereof, and yet is not so indeed; so I pray God, that we have not rather been figures of bishops, bearing the name and title of pastors and bishops before men, than that we have in deed diligently fed the little flock of Christ with the sweet and wholesome pasture of his true and lively word.[12]

Finally, the confrontational, quibbling tone of the book is somewhat redeemed by its conclusion, and a passage in which Cranmer, affirming the presence of Christ for all believers at the Communion, lets his prose take flight. As Diarmaid MacCulloch says, it is an almost mystical passage, of theological beauty and literary elegance.[13]

For what ought to be more certain and known to all christian people, than that Christ died once, and but once, for the redemption of the world? And what can be more true, than that his only death is our life? And what can be more comfortable to a penitent sinner, that is sorry for his sin, and returneth to God in his heart and whole mind, than to know that Christ dischargeth him of the heavy load of his sin, and taketh the burden upon his own back?

And furthermore, when we hear Christ speak unto us with his own mouth, and show himself to be seen with our eyes, in such sort as is convenient for him of us in this mortal life to be heard and seen; what comfort can we have more? The minister of the church speaketh unto us God's own words, which we must take as spoken from God's own mouth, because that from his mouth it came, and his word it is, and not the minister's. Likewise, when he ministereth to our sights Christ's holy sacraments, we must think Christ crucified and presented before our eyes, because the sacraments so represent him, and be his sacraments, and not the priest's: as in baptism we must think, that as the priest putteth his hand to the child outwardly, and washeth him with water, so we must think that God putteth to his hand inwardly, and washeth the infant with the Holy Spirit; and moreover, that Christ himself cometh down upon the child, and apparelleth him with his own self: and as at the Lord's holy table the priest distributeth wine and bread to feed the body, so we must think that inwardly by faith we see Christ feeding both body and soul to eternal life. What comfort can be devised any more in this world for a christian man?[14]

12 Cranmer, *Writings and disputations*, p. 275.
13 MacCulloch, *Thomas Cranmer*, p. 615.
14 Cranmer, *Writings and disputations*, p. 366.

6

Facing Death: 1553–6

Ah, how the sweet words ring their beauty:
'it is meet, right, and our bounden duty.'
But will you sing it with unchanged faces
When God shall change the times and places?[1]

The death of the teenage Edward VI in July 1553 dashed both the great progress of the Reformation in England and the high hopes of its architects for more and further change. Despite the best efforts of the Council to bypass Edward's half-sister Mary's legitimate claim to the throne and install his cousin Lady Jane Grey whose Christianity was reassuringly Protestant in her place, the people rose up against their attempt to subvert the succession of Henry VIII's rightful heir. Mary had made plain her intention to reinstate both the papal supremacy and traditional Catholic practice and observance in England; so it was with agonizing irony, and a sense of foreboding we may only guess at, that the King's godfather, Archbishop Thomas Cranmer, conducted the funeral service with the 1552 rite from the *Book of Common Prayer*. Within weeks, the rite was defunct, and those who had crafted and implemented it were removed from office. Some also lost their lives.

Mary had also made plain her intention severely to punish those who had tried to ignore her father's clear wishes in the succession and who had, in her view, mired the realm deep in heresy and false teaching. Much reviled in later historical understanding, she had herself suffered the worst of times during and after the prosecution of her father's 'Great Matter', in savage and very personal ways: separated from her mother, refused permission to visit her as she died, declared illegitimate as a child and then forced to stand by while her much younger brother asserted his growing confidence, even brashness, in religious

---

1 From Charles Williams, *Thomas Cranmer of Canterbury*, reprinted in E. M. Browne (ed.), *Four Modern Verse Plays* (Harmondsworth: Penguin, 1964), p. 173.

affairs against her. That she developed a frail psychological state was therefore hardly surprising; but she was not the monster of later myth. For all that, her animus against those who had led the changes of the last 20 years and the attempt to marginalize her was bitter. Thus, the leaders of the Council were soon arrested, and the Lady Jane and her husband, the son of the Duke of Northumberland, killed along with Northumberland himself. Cranmer himself at first was spared, as the regime dealt with its political foes; then after his stubborn refusal to allow the reinstatement of the Mass, he was imprisoned: first, in the Tower of London, during which time he was convicted of his share in the treason against Mary in the succession plot, and then subsequently in the 'Bocardo' jail in Oxford, where he was tried for heresy and eventually burned in March 1556. With bitter irony, and perhaps with anxious foresight, Cranmer had written to Stephen Gardiner in the *Answer* just months before Mary's accession that the truth 'hath been persecuted by the papists with fire and fagot, and should be so yet still if you might have your own will'.[2] Now, his own life was to be given up in that manner.

As related earlier,[3] Cranmer's punishment under the Marian authorities was long and tortuous, because of the process of resubmission to Roman authority which the Queen desired to follow. Three letters follow which illustrate this: the first is to William Cecil (later Lord Burghley, the architect of the Elizabethan renaissance), an anxious, cautious epistle before Cranmer's arrest in September 1553. The second was written to the Queen herself, lamenting his failure to oppose the plot to sideline her, which he genuinely seems to have disliked because of his deep loyalty to the Tudor family line, and, more surprisingly, asking to open his mind to her personally about the state of the English Church, something she was never remotely likely to grant. The third is to a Mrs Wilkinson, advising her as a Protestant to flee the trials of Marian England and not see such self-preservation as faithless desertion. It is a beautiful, gentle, pastoral letter which she seems to have heeded. Cranmer himself, of course, remained to face his destiny.

---

2 Thomas Cranmer, *The works of Thomas Cranmer, Archbishop of Canterbury, Martyr 1556*, 2 vols, ed. John Edmund Cox (Cambridge: Parker Society 1844–6), vol. 1, *Writings and disputations, relative to the sacrament of the Lord's Supper*, p. 224.

3 See Introduction, pp. 15–18.

To Cecil

After my very hearty recommendations; yesternight I heard reported that Mr. Cheke is indicted: I pray you heartily, if you know any thing thereof, to send me knowledge, and whereupon he is indicted. I had great trust that he should be one of them that should feel the queen's great mercy and pardon, as one who hath been none of the great doers in this matter against her: and my trust is not yet gone, except it be for his earnestness in religion: for the which if he suffer, blessed is he of God, that suffereth for his sake, howsoever the world judge of him. For what ought we to care for the judgement of the world, when God absolveth us? But, alas! If any means could be made for him, or for my lord Russel, it were not to be omitted, nor in any wise neglected. But I am utterly destitute both of counsel in this matter and of power, being in the same condemnation that they be. But that only thing which I can do, I shall not cease to do; and that is only to pray for them and for myself, with all other that be now in adversity. When I saw you at the court, I would fain have talked with you, but I durst not: nevertheless, if you could find a time to come over to me, I would gladly commune with you.

To Queen Mary

Most lamentably mourning and moaning himself unto your highness, Thomas Cranmer, although unworthy either to write or speak unto your highness, yet having no person that I know to be mediator for me, and knowing your pitiful ears ready to hear all pitiful complaints, and seeing so many before to have felt your abundant clemency in like case, am now constrained most lamentably, and with most penitent and sorrowful heart, to ask mercy and pardon for my heinous folly and offence, in consenting and following the testament and last will of our late sovereign lord king Edward VI your grace's brother: which will, God he knoweth, I never liked: nor never anything grieved me so much that your grace's brother did. And if by any means it had been in me to have letted the making of that will, I would have done it . . . I desired to talk with the king's majesty alone, but I could not be suffered, and I failed of my purpose.

I submit myself most humbly unto your majesty, acknowledging mine offence with most grievous and sorrowful heart, and beseeching your mercy and pardon: which my heart giveth me shall not be denied unto me, being granted before to so many, which travailed not so much to dissuade both the king and his council as I did.

Now as concerning the estate of religion, as it is used in this realm of England at this present, if it please your highness to license me, I would gladly write my mind unto your majesty. I will never, God willing, be author of sedition, to move subjects from the obedience of their heads and rulers: which is an offence most detestable. If I have uttered my mind to your majesty, being a christian queen and governor of this realm, (of whom I am most assuredly persuaded, that your gracious intent is, above all other regards, to prefer God's true word, his honour and glory,) if I have uttered, I say, my mind unto your majesty, then I shall think myself discharged. For it lieth not in me, but in your grace only, to see the reformation of things that be amiss. To private subjects[4] it appertaineth not to reform things, but quietly to suffer that they cannot amend. Yet nevertheless to show your majesty my mind in things pertaining unto God, methink it my duty, knowing that I do, and considering the place which in times past I have occupied. Yet I will not presume thereunto without your grace's pleasure first known, and your license obtained: whereof I most humbly prostrate to the ground do beseech your majesty; and I shall not cease daily to pray to Almighty God for the good preservation of your majesty from all enemies bodily and ghostly, and for the increase of all goodness heavenly and earthly, during my life, as I do and will do, whatsoever come of me.

To Mrs Wilkinson

The true comforter in all distress is only God, through his Son Jesus Christ; and whosoever hath him, hath company enough, although he were in a wilderness all alone. And he that hath twenty thousand in his company, if God be absent, he is in a miserable wilderness and desolation. In him is all comfort, and without him is none. Wherefore, I beseech you, seek your dwelling there, where as you may truly and rightly serve God, and dwell in him, and have him ever dwelling in you. What can be so heavy a burden as an unquiet conscience, to be in such a place as a man cannot be suffered to serve God in Christ's true religion? If you be loth to part from your kin

---

4 At the time of writing, Cranmer was in a strange limbo, relieved of the legal exercise of his office as Archbishop, but not officially deprived until the papal obedience could be restored and the due (in Mary's mind) ecclesiastical procedures observed.

and friends, remember, that Christ calleth them his mother, sisters, and brothers, that do his Father's will. Where we find therefore God truly honoured according to his will, there we can lack neither friend nor kin.

If you be loth to depart for the slandering of God's word, remember, that Christ, when his hour was not yet come, departed out of his country into Samaria, to avoid the malice of the scribes and Pharisees; and commanded his apostles, that if they were pursued in one place, they should fly to another. And was not Paul let down by a basket out at a window, to avoid the persecution of Aretas? And what wisdom and policy he used from time to time, to escape the malice of his enemies, the Acts of the Apostles do declare. And after the same sort did the other apostles. Mary, when it came to such a point, that they could no longer escape danger of the persecutors of God's true religion; then they showed themselves, that their flying before came not of fear, but of godly wisdom to do more good, and that they would not rashly, without urgent necessity, offer themselves to death; which had been but a temptation of God. Yet, when they were apprehended, and could no longer avoid, then they stood boldly to the profession of Christ: then they showed how little they passed of death; how much they feared God more than men; how much they loved and preferred the eternal life to come above this short and miserable life.

Wherefore I exhort you, as well by Christ's commandment as by the example of him and his apostles, to withdraw yourself from the malice of your and God's enemies, into some place where God is most truly served: which is no slandering of the truth, but a preserving of yourself to God and the truth, and to the society and comfort of Christ's little flock. And that you will do, do it with speed, lest by your own folly you fall into the persecutors' hands. And the Lord send his Holy Spirit to lead and guide you, wheresoever you go![5]

The poignant drama of Cranmer's last weeks and days are unlikely ever to be forgotten, thanks to the work of the martyrologist John Foxe. Foxe's account of the final events of the Archbishop's life, though clearly biased in their intent, still offer a reliable and moving insight into both the pathos and the human dignity with which these moments

---

5 Thomas Cranmer, *The works of Thomas Cranmer, Archbishop of Canterbury, Martyr 1556*, 2 vols, ed. John Edmund Cox (Cambridge: Parker Society, 1844–4), vol. 2, *Miscellaneous writings and letters*, pp. 441–5.

were imbued. Here then are Foxe's accounts of the two final stages in Cranmer's end, after what must have seemed the interminable time of his disputations with scholars, his separation from Ridley and Latimer until their deaths, and his final months of incarceration, persuasion and interrogation: first, Cranmer's 'degradation' from archiepiscopal status in Christ Church, Oxford, and then the dramatic events of his last day on earth, which culminated in his renunciation of his recantations. Restored to his Protestant loyalties, Cranmer perished boldly and defiantly, in a manner that Foxe soon realized was the stuff of legend.

[A] letter or sentence definitive of the Pope was dated about the first day of January, and was delivered here in England about the middle of February. Upon the receipt of which letters another session was appointed for the Archbishop to appear the 14 day of February, before certain Commissions directed down by the Queen, the chief whereof was the Bishop of Ely Doctor Thirlby.

Concerning which Doctor Thirlby, by the way here is to be noted, that albeit he was not the said Archbishop's household Chaplain, yet he was so familiarly acquainted with him, so dearly beloved, so inwardly accepted and advanced of him (not like a Chaplain, but rather like a natural brother) that there was never anything in the Archbishop's house so dear, were it plate, jewel, horse, maps, books, or any thing else, but if Thirlby did never so little commend it, (a subtle kind of begging) the Archbishop by and by, either gave it to him, or shortly sent it after him to his house. So greatly was the Archbishop enamoured with him, that whosoever would obtain anything of him, most commonly would make their way before by Dr. Thirlby. Which bymatter of the said Doctor Thirlby, I thought here to recite, not so much to rebraid the man with the voice of unthankfulness, as chiefly and only for this, to admonish him of old benefits received whereby he may the better remember his old benefactor, and so to favour the cause and quarrel of him whom he was so singularly bounden unto.

With the said Doctor Thirlby bishop of Ely, was also assigned in the same Commission Doctor Bonner Bishop of London, which two coming to Oxford upon S. Valentines day, as the Pope's delegates, with a new commission from Rome, by the virtue thereof commanded the Archbishop aforesaid to come before them, in the quire of Christ Church before the high altar, where they sitting (according to their manner) in their 'pontificalibus', first began as the fashion is, to read their Commission: wherein was contained, how that in the Court of Rome all things being indifferently examined, both the articles laid to his charge, with the answers made unto them and witnesses examined on both parts, and counsel heard as well on the King and Queen's behalf his accusers, as on the behalf of T. Cranmer, the party guilty, so that he wanted nothing appertaining to his necessary defence, etc.

Which foresaid Commission, as it was in reading, 'O lord' said the Archbishop, 'what lies be these, that I being continually in prison, and never could be suffered to have counsel or advocate at home, should produce witness and appoint my counsel at Rome? God must needs punish this open and shameless lying.' They read on the Commission which came from the Pope . . . supplying all manner of defects in law or process, committed in dealing with the Archbishop, and giving them full authority to proceed to the deprivation and degradation of him, and so upon excommunication to deliver him up to the secular power.

When the commission was read thus, they proceeding thereupon, to his degradation, first clothed and disguised him: putting on him a surplice, and then an Alb: after that the vestment of a Subdeacon, and every other furniture, as a Priest ready to Mass. When they had apparelled him so far: 'What,' said he, 'I think I shall say Mass.' 'Yea,' said Cosins one of Bonner's Chaplains, 'my Lord, I trust to see you say Mass, for all this.' 'Do you so?' quoth he, 'that shall you never see, nor I will never do it.' Then they invested him in all manner of Robes of a Bishop and Archbishop, as he is at his installing, saving that as every thing then is most rich and costly, so every thing in this was of canvas and old clothes, with a Mitre and a Pall of the same suit down upon him in mockery, and then the crozier staff was put in his hand.

After all this done & finished, they began then to bustle toward his disgrading, and first to take from him his Crozier staff out of his hands, which he held fast, and refused to deliver, & withal imitating the example of Martin Luther, pulled an Appeal out of his left sleeve under the wrist, which he there and then delivered unto them, saying: 'I appeal to the next general Council: and herein I have comprehended my cause and form of it, which I desire may be admitted': and prayed divers of the standers by, by name to be witnesses.

This appeal being put up to the Bishop of Ely, he said: 'My Lord, our Commission is to proceed against you . . . and therefore we cannot admit it.'

'Why' (quoth he) 'then you do me the more wrong: for my case is not as every private man's case. The matter is between the Pope and me immediately, and none otherwise: and I think no man ought to be a judge in his own cause.'

'Well' (quoth Ely) 'if it may be admitted, it shall,' and so received it of him. And then began he to persuade earnestly with the Archbishop to consider his state, and to weigh it well, while there was time to do him good, promising to become a suitor to the King and Queen for him: and so protested his great love and friendship that had been between them, heartily weeping, so that for a time he could not go on with his tale. After going forward, he earnestly affirmed, that if it had not been the King and Queen's commandment, whom he could not deny, else no worldly commodity should have made him to have done it, concluding that to be one of the sorrowfullest things that ever happened unto him. The Archbishop gently seeming to comfort him, said, he was very well content withal: and so proceeded they to his degradation.

Here then to be short, when they came to take off his Pall (which is a solemn vesture of an Archbishop) then said he: 'Which of you hath a Pall, to take off my Pall?' Which imported as much as they being his inferiors, could not disgrade him. Whereunto one of them said, in that they were but Bishops, they were his inferiors, and not competent judges: but being the pope's Delegates, they might take his Pall, and so they did: and so proceeding, took every thing in order from him, as it was put on. Then a Barber clipped his hair round about, and the Bishop scraped the tops of his fingers where he had been anointed, wherein Bishop Bonner behaved himself as roughly and unmannerly, as the other Bishop was to him soft and gentle. Whiles they were thus doing, 'All this' (quoth the Archbishop) 'needed not: I had myself done with this gear long ago.'

Last of all, they stripped him out of his gown into his jacket, and put upon him a poor yeoman Beadle's gown, full bare and nearly worn, and as evil favouredly made, as one might lightly see, and a town's man's cap on his head, and so delivered him to the secular power.

After this pageant of degradation, and all was finished, then spake Lord Bonner, saying to him: 'Now are you no Lord any more.' And so whensoever he spake to the people of him (as he was continually barking against him) ever he used this term: 'This Gentleman here', etc.

And thus with great compassion and pity of every man in this evil-favoured gown was he carried to prison. Whom there followed a gentleman of Gloucestershire with the archbishop's own gown, who standing by, and being thought to be toward one of the Bishops, had it delivered to him: who by the way talking with him, said: 'the Bishop of Ely protested his friendship with tears.' 'Yea' (said he) 'he might have used a great deal more friendship toward me, and never have been the worse thought on, for I have well deserved it': and going into the prison up with him, asked him if he would drink. Who answered him, saying: if he had a piece of saltfish, that he had better will to eat: for he had been that day somewhat troubled with this matter, and had eaten little, but now that it is past, my heart (said he) is well quieted.

Whereupon the gentleman said, he would give him money with all his heart, for he was able to do it. But he being one toward the law, and fearing M. Farmer's case, durst therefore give him nothing, but gave money to the bailiffs that stood by, and said, that if they were good men, they would bestow it on him (for my Lord of Canterbury had not one penny in his purse to help him) and so left him, my Lord bidding him earnestly farewell, commending himself to his prayers and all his friends. That night this gentleman was stayed by Bonner and Ely, for giving him this money: and but by the help of friends, he had been sent up to the Council. Such was the cruelty and iniquity of the time, that men could not do good without punishment.

21 March 1556

Soon after, about 9 of the clock, the Lord Williams, Sir Thomas Bridges, Sir John Browne, and the other justices with certain other noble men, that were sent of the Queen's council, came to Oxford with a great train of waiting men. Also of the other multitude on every side, (as is wont in such a matter) was made a great concourse and greater expectation. For first of all, they that were of the Pope's side, were in great hope that day to hear something of Cranmer that should stablish the vanity of their opinion: the other part which were endued with a better mind, could not yet doubt, that he which by continual study and labour, for so many years had set forth the doctrine of the gospel, either would or could now in the last Act of his life forsake his part. Briefly, as every man's will inclined, either to this part or to that, so according to the diversity of their desires, every man wished and hoped for. And yet because in an uncertain thing the certainty could be known of none what would be the end: all their minds were hanging between hope and doubt. So that the greater the expectation was in so doubtful a matter, the more was the multitude that were gathered thither to hear and behold.

In this so great frequence and expectation, Cranmer at length cameth from the prison Bocardo, unto St. Mary's church (because it was a foul and a rainy day) the chief church in the university, in this order. The Mayor went before, next him the Aldermen in their place and degree, after them was Cranmer brought between two friars, which mumbling to and fro certain Psalms in the streets, answered one another until they came to the Church door, and there they began the song of Simeon, Nunc Dimittis, and entering into the Church, the Psalm-saying Friars brought him to his standing, and there left him.

There was a stage set up over against the pulpit, of a mean height from the ground, where Cranmer had his standing, waiting until Cole made him ready to his Sermon. The lamentable case and sight of that man gave a sorrowful spectacle to all Christian eyes that beheld him. He that late was Archbishop, Metropolitan, and Primate of England, and the King's Privy Councillor, being now in a bare and ragged gown, and ill-favouredly clothed, with an old square cap, exposed to the contempt of all men, did admonish men not only of his own calamity, but also of their state and fortune. For who would not pity his case, and bewail his fortune, and might not fear his own chance, to see such a Prelate, so grave a Councillor, and of so long continued honour, after so many dignities, in his old years to be deprived of his estate, adjudged to die, and in so painful a death to end his life, and now presently from such fresh ornaments, to descend to such vile and ragged apparel?

In this habit, when he had stood a good space upon the stage, turning to a pillar near adjoining thereunto, he lifted up his hands to heaven, and prayed unto God once or twice: till at the length Dr. Cole coming into the pulpit, [began] his sermon.

Cranmer in all this meantime, with what great grief of mind he stood hearing this Sermon, the outward shows of his body and countenance did better express, than any man can declare: one while lifting up his hands and eyes unto heaven, and then again for shame letting them down to the earth. A man might have seen the very image and shape of perfect sorrow lively in him expressed. More then twenty several times the tears gushed out abundantly, dropped down marvellously from his Fatherly face. They which were present, do testify that they never saw in any child more tears, than brast out from him at that time, all the Sermon while: but specially when he recited his Prayer before the people. It is marvellous what commiseration and pity moved all men's hearts, that beheld so heavy a countenance, and such abundance of tears in an old man of so reverend dignity.

Cole after he had ended his Sermon, called back the people that were ready to depart, to prayers. 'Brethren', (said he) 'lest any man should doubt of this man's earnest conversion and repentance, you shall hear him speak before you, and therefore I pray you master Cranmer, that you will now perform that you promised not long ago: namely, that you would openly express the true and undoubted profession of your faith, that you may take away all suspicion from men, and that all men may understand that you are a Catholic indeed.'

'I will do it', (said the Archbishop) 'and with a good will': who by and by rising up, and putting off his cap, began to speak thus unto the people:

'I desire you well beloved brethren in the Lord, that you will pray to God for me, to forgive me my sins, which above all men, both in number and greatness, I have committed: But among all the rest, there is one offence, which of all at this time doth vex and trouble me, whereof in process of my talk you shall hear more in his proper place', and then putting his hand into his bosom, he drew forth his Prayer, which he recited to the people in this sense.

'Good Christian people, my dearly beloved brethren and sisters in Christ, I beseech you most heartily to pray for me to almighty God, that he will forgive me all my sins and offences, which be many, without number, and great above measure. But yet one thing grieveth my conscience more than all the rest, whereof God willing, I intend to speak more hereafter. But how great and how many soever my sins be, I beseech you to pray God of his mercy to pardon and forgive them all.' And here kneeling down, he said:

'O Father of heaven: O son of God redeemer of the world: O holy Ghost, three persons and one God, have mercy upon me most wretched caitiff[6] and miserable sinner. I have offended both against heaven and earth, more than my tongue can express. Whither then may I go, or whither should I fly? To heaven I may be ashamed to lift up mine eyes, and in earth I find no place of refuge or succour. To thee therefore (O Lord) do I run: to thee do I humble myself saying, O Lord my God, my sin be great, but yet have mercy upon me for thy great mercy. The great mystery that God became man, was not wrought for little or few offences. Thou diddest not give thy son (O heavenly father) unto death for small sins only, but for all the greatest sins of the world, so that the sinner return to thee with his whole heart, as I do here at this present. Wherefore have mercy on me O

---

6 A coward; one lacking courage.

God, whose property is always to have mercy, have mercy upon me O Lord, for thy great mercy. I crave nothing for mine own merits, but for thy name's sake, that it may be hallowed thereby, and for thy dear son Jesus Christ's sake. And now therefore, Our Father of heaven, hallowed be thy name, etc.' And then he rising, said:

'Every man (good people) desireth at that time of their death to give some good exhortation, that other may remember the same before their death, & be the better thereby: so I beseech God grant me grace, that I may speak some thing at this my departing, whereby God may be glorified, and you edified.

'First, it is an heavy case to see that so many folk be so much doted upon the love of this false world, and so careful for it, that of the love of God, or the world to come, they seem to care very little or nothing. Therefore this shall be my first exhortation, that you set not your minds over much upon this glosing[7] world, but upon God and upon the world to come: and to learn to know what this lesson meaneth, which St. John teacheth, that the love of this world is hatred against God.

'The second exhortation is, that next under God you obey your King and Queen[8] willingly and gladly, without murmuring or grudging: not for fear of them only, but much more for the fear of God: knowing that they be God's ministers, appointed by God to rule and govern you: and therefore whosoever resisteth them, resisteth the ordinance of God.

'The third exhortation is, that you love altogether like brethren and sisters. For alas, pity it is to see what contention and hatred one Christian man beareth to another, not taking each other as brother and sister, but rather as strangers and mortal enemies. But I pray you learn and bear well away this one lesson, to do good unto all men, as much as in you lieth, and to hurt no man, no more than you would hurt your own natural loving brother or sister. For this you may be sure of, that whosoever hateth any person, and goeth about maliciously to hinder or hurt him, surely, and without all doubt God is not with that man, although he think himself never so much in God's favour.

---

7 Flattering, false.

8 Queen Mary had married King Phillip II of Spain on 25 July 1554 and ceded joint rule of the kingdom to him, prompting considerable disquiet among her subjects; Cranmer makes no capital from the unpopular match here, on the contrary encouraging a characteristically staunch view of the royal supremacy, which probably in fact would have angered Mary even more than an attack on her foreign husband.

'The fourth exhortation shall be to them that have great substance and riches of this world, that they will well consider and weigh three sayings of the Scripture. One is of our Saviour Christ himself, who saith: It is hard for a rich man to enter into the kingdom of heaven. A sore saying, and yet spoken of him that knoweth the truth. The second is of St. John, whose saying is this: He that hath the substance of this world, and seeth his brother in necessity, and shutteth up his mercy from him, how can he say that he loveth God? The third is of St. James, who speaketh to the covetous rich man after this manner: Weep you and howl for the misery that shall come upon you: your riches do rot, your clothes be moth-eaten, your gold and silver doth canker and rust, and their rust shall bear witness against you, and consume you like fire: you gather a hoard or treasure of God's indignation against the last day.

'Let them that be rich, ponder well these three sentences: for if they had occasion to show their charity, they have it now at this present, the poor people being so many, and victuals so dear.

'And now, for as much as I am come to the last end of my life, whereupon hangeth all my life past, and all my life to come, either to live with my master Christ forever in joy, or else to be in pain forever, with wicked Devils in hell, and I see before mine eyes presently either heaven ready to receive me, or else hell ready to swallow me up: I shall therefore declare unto you my very faith how I believe, without any colour or dissimulation: for now is no time to dissemble, whatsoever I have said or written in time past.

'First, I believe in God the Father almighty, maker of heaven and earth, etc. And I believe every Article of the Catholic faith, every word and sentence taught by our Saviour Jesus Christ, his Apostles and Prophets, in the new and old Testament.

'And now I come to the great thing, that so much troubleth my conscience more than any thing that ever I did or said in my whole life, and that is the setting abroad of a writing contrary to the truth: which now here I renounce and refuse as things written with my hand, contrary to the truth which I thought in my heart, and written for fear of death, and to save my life if it might be, and that is, all such bills and papers which I have written or signed with my hand since my degradation: wherein I have written many things untrue. And for asmuch as my hand offended, writing contrary to my heart, my hand shall first be punished therefore: for may I come to the fire, it shall be first burned. And as for the Pope, I refuse him as Christ's enemy and Antichrist, with all his false doctrine.

'And as for the sacrament, I believe as I have taught in my book against the Bishop of Winchester,[9] the which my book teacheth so true a doctrine of the sacrament, that it shall stand at the last day before the judgement of God, where the Papistical doctrine contrary thereto, shall be ashamed to show her face.'

Here the standers by were all astonished, marvelled, were amazed, did look one upon another, whose expectation he had so notably deceived. Some began to admonish him of his recantation, and to accuse him of falsehood.

Briefly, it was a world to see the doctors beguiled of so great an hope. I think there was never cruelty more notably or better in time deluded and deceived. For it is not to be doubted but they looked for a glorious victory, and a perpetual triumph by this man's retractation.

Who as soon as they heard these things, began to let down their ears, to rage, fret, and fume: and so much the more, because they could not revenge their grief: for they could now no longer threaten or hurt him. For the most miserable man in the world can die but once: and where as of necessity he must needs die that day, though the papists had been never so well pleased: now being never so much offended with him, yet could he not be twice killed of them. And so when they could do nothing else unto him, yet lest they should say nothing, they ceased not to object unto him his falsehood and dissimulation.

Unto which accusation he answered: 'Ah my masters' (quoth he) 'do not you take it so. Always since I lived hitherto, I have been a hater of falsehood, and a lover of simplicity, and never before this time have I dissembled': and in saying this, all the tears that remained in his body, appeared in his eyes. And when he began to speak more of the sacrament and of the papacy, some of them began to cry out, yelp, and bawl, and specially Cole cried out upon him: 'Stop the heretic's mouth, and take him away.'

And then Cranmer being pulled down from the stage, was led to the fire, accompanied with those Friars, vexing, troubling, and threatening him most cruelly. 'What madness' (say they) 'hath brought thee again into this error, by which thou wilt draw innumerable souls with thee into hell?' To whom he answered nothing, but directed all his talk to the people, saving that to one troubling him in the way, he spake and exhorted him to get him home to his study, and apply his

---

9 The *Answer*, which of course also included much of the text of the earlier *Defence*.

book diligently, saying if he did diligently call upon God, by reading more he should get knowledge. But the other Spanish barker, raging and foaming, was almost out of his wits, always having this in his mouth: 'Non fecisti? diddest thou it not?'

But when he came to the place where the holy Bishops and Martyrs of God, Hugh Latimer and Ridley were burnt before him for the confession of the truth, kneeling down, he prayed to God, and not long tarrying in his prayers, putting off his garments to his shirt, he prepared himself to death. His shirt was made long down to his feet. His feet were bare. Likewise his head, when both his caps were off, was so bare, that one hair could not be seen upon it. His beard was long and thick, covering his face with marvellous gravity. Such a countenance of gravity moved the hearts both of his friends and of his enemies.

Then the Spanish Friars John and Richard, of whom mention was made before, began to exhort him and play their parts with him afresh, but with vain and lost labour, Cranmer with steadfast purpose abiding in the profession of his doctrine, gave his hand to certain old men, and other that stood by, bidding them farewell . . . Then was an iron chain tied about Cranmer, whom when they perceived to be more steadfast than that he could be moved from his sentence, they commanded the fire to be set unto him.

And when the wood was kindled, and the fire began to burn near him, stretching out his arm, he put his right hand into the flame: which he held so steadfast and immovable (saving that once with the same hand he wiped his face) that all men might see his hand burned before his body was touched. His body did so abide the burning of the flame with such constancy and steadfastness, that standing always in one place without moving of his body, he seemed to move no more than the stake to which he was bound: his eyes were lifted up into heaven, and oftentimes he repeated his unworthy right hand, so long as his voice would suffer him: and using often the words of Steven, 'Lord Jesus receive my spirit,' in the greatness of the flame, he gave up the Ghost.[10]

We end, however, with the very words of Cranmer himself, the last letter of his which survives, treasured by its recipient in continental Europe and kept among his papers for posterity. Although it is likely

---

10 Extract taken from John Foxe, *The Unabridged Acts and Monuments Online* or *TAMO* (1583 edition, pp. 1181–8) (HRI Online Publications, Sheffield, 2011). Available from: http//www.johnfoxe.org [Accessed: 11 August 2011].

that this letter was written around a year before Cranmer's final trial and death, it is a beautiful encapsulation of Cranmer's fortitude and faith, in the face of the most dreadful of circumstances. It acts too as a final illustration of how deep and heartfelt were Cranmer's connections to the leading Reformers across the sea, that he cherished contact with them, even as his dreams of the fulfilment of his life's purpose in the full reformation of the English Church faded and died.

To Peter Martyr

After much health in Christ our Saviour. As letters are then only necessary, when the messenger is either not sufficiently discreet, or is unacquainted with the circumstances we wish to communicate, or not thought worthy to be entrusted with secrets; and since by the goodness of God the bearer of this has fallen in my way, a man, as you know, of signal discretion, most faithful in all matters entrusted to him, exceedingly attached to us both, and possessing an entire acquaintance with the circumstances of our country, from whose mouth you may learn all that has taken place here;[11] I have not thought it needful to write to you at more length, especially as letters are wont to occasion so much danger and mischief. Yet I have not deemed it right to pass over this one thing, which I have learned by experience, namely, that God never shines forth more brightly, and pours out the beams of his mercy and consolation, or of strength and firmness of spirit, more clearly or impressively upon the minds of his people, than when they are under the most extreme pain and distress, both of mind and body, that he may then more especially show himself to be the God of his people, when he seems to have altogether forsaken them; then raising them up when they think he is bringing them down, and laying them low; then glorifying them, when he is thought to be counfounding them; then quickening them, when he is thought to be destroying them. So that we may say with Paul, 'When I am weak, then I am strong; and if I must needs glory, I will glory in my infirmities, in prisons, in revilings, in distress, in persecutions, in sufferings for Christ.' I pray God to grant that I may endure to the end![12]

---

11 The bearer of this letter was possibly John Jewel, later Bishop of Salisbury under Elizabeth I and a key figure in the shaping and defining of the Elizabethan religious settlement.

12 Cranmer, *Miscellaneous writings*, pp. 457–8.

Afterlife

Executed as a traitor and a heretic, no grave marks the final resting place of Archbishop Thomas Cranmer. In the middle of Broad Street, Oxford, outside Balliol College, a plain cross made of yellow bricks marks the site of his burning. Around the corner, there is a Gothic Victorian memorial to him, Latimer and Ridley, erected 300 years after their deaths mainly to be a rebuke to the reintroduction of Catholic elements in the Church of England; these days, it is usually the site of apocalyptic street preaching (of which Cranmer would strongly have disapproved) rather than any real reflection on his legacy. In the chapel of Jesus College, Cambridge, a simple relief of him adorns one transept wall, above the simple word: Cranmer. It is almost as if his *alma mater* did not quite know how to memorialize its martyr son either. In his home village of Aslockton, a stained-glass window in the church commemorates him, but not perhaps as noticeably as the naming of a pub in his honour. It is a very everyday, English way to remember an English saint, and certainly guarantees a greater immortality than monuments in church.

Of course, Cranmer's real legacy is the Church of England and its global child, the Anglican Communion. Within it, his spiritual heirs claim his influence in diverse and often uninformed ways. Some are lulled by the soothing ancient rhythms of the language of the Prayer Book into believing Cranmer to have been opposed to all change or innovation in liturgical matters. They fight against novelty in modern worship on the basis that he would have disapproved of it, ignorant of how extreme a break with the past the 1549 Prayer Book represented. Others attempt to find in him a champion of 'Catholic' elements in the Church, missing his Reformed radicalism. In 1707, the Revd Edward Stephens went so far as to blame Cranmer for conniving at the 1552 *Book of Common Prayer*, which left the Church of England with a 'bastard' eucharistic theology.[1] Far from merely conniving at the book, Cranmer

---

1 Reported in Diarmaid MacCulloch, *Tudor Church Militant* (London: Penguin, 1999), p. 172.

actively shaped and pushed for its content; its theology was his own, as the Forty-Two Articles also make clear. Evangelicals rightly sense in him a theological ally, but often overlook and underestimate his gradualism, his generosity and gentleness towards those with whom he disagreed, and his deep pastoral concern for all the Church of England's communicants, whatever their religious convictions. Many of those who do not misappropriate his role in the shaping of the Church simply and unfairly ignore it. Cranmer is not revered by Anglicans as is Luther by those who stand in his theological tradition or Wesley by Methodists. And yet, as Edward Carpenter has stated, despite being overshadowed by Cromwell in his early years as Archbishop, Cranmer's influence on the nascent Church of England was critical and pivotal: no-one else 'left the imprint of his personality more indelibly upon it'.[2] One major reason for his comparative neglect in this regard is perhaps the rather convoluted history and the ongoing evolution of the Church after his death, which has sometimes made it difficult precisely to trace his legacy. For all that, the stamp of his character does indeed still run very deep.

Thomas Cranmer's other godchild Elizabeth I, the child of Anne Boleyn, succeeded Mary in 1558. The religious settlement which she forged in the ensuing years defined the English Church for centuries, largely through the Queen's tenacious and stubborn espousal of its principles, which by the end of her long reign had rooted themselves firmly. Her regime notably retreated from the place to which the English Reformation had arrived by 1553, however, softening the eucharistic theology, reducing and reframing the articles of religion, and charting a 'middle way' that remains an ecclesiastical oddity, a moderate Protestant Church set in ancient Catholic structures. Elizabeth's godfather would have been no happier with the result than were many of her senior churchmen, since Cranmer had set a much bolder course himself during Edward's reign: but the result was still recognizably his Church. The reissued prayer book of 1559 was still basically his work, amended and altered, as it was in its final form of 1662. Thus, his language became embedded in the English-speaking world as generations gathered for worship and to mark the times of their lives. On the three-hundred-and-fiftieth anniversary of the publication of this final version, it is important to remember the extent to which its services, and perhaps especially those for Morning and Evening Prayer and for marriage and burial, continue to shape the expression of human spirituality and influence all subsequent liturgy.

---

2 Edward Carpenter and Adrian Hastings, *Cantuar: The Archbishops in Their Office* (London: Mowbray, 1997), p. 138.

If the theology of the Anglican Communion thus shifted away from Cranmer's original trajectory in the 1550s and 1560s, other essential elements of his character seem to remain. One of the hardest tasks for the editor of a volume such as this one is to read through all the pages of polemical material which Reformation disputes inevitably bring with them. Much of Cranmer's work on the Eucharist and many passages in the homilies take their fire from his passionate rejection of the papacy and the medieval traditions of the Catholic Church; I have had to edit these sections ruthlessly to produce a more edifying and less tiresomely negative book, and to leave what I hope are kernels of more uplifting reflection. And yet, for all that, Cranmer emerges as someone decidedly more generous than his peers. The disputes of the sixteenth century were always bitter, and the custom of the time was for the use of fierce and uncompromising language on all sides. One does not, however, encounter the embarrassingly scatological rants of Luther or Thomas More in Cranmer's work; and where Luther's writings on the Jews are shameful and make a huge and sickening contribution to the centuries of Christian anti-Jewishness which culminated in the horrors of the *Shoah*,[3] Cranmer seems to have read the letters to the Romans and Hebrews rather more carefully than Luther, in being able to state of the Jews in the *Homily of Faith*:

> God gave them the grace to be his children, as he doth us now. But now, by the coming of our saviour Christ we have received more abundantly the Spirit of God in our hearts, whereby we may conceive a greater faith, and a surer trust, than many of them had. But in effect they and we be all one: we have the same faith that they had in God, and they the same that we have.[4]

Similarly, in his efforts to spare opponents and comfort those of whom he disapproved, Cranmer's humanity shines through repeatedly. He was a man of his time: but his essential compassion and generosity and the breadth of his empathy entered the DNA of Anglicanism in its liturgy, in the magnanimity of Queen Elizabeth, refusing to make windows onto human souls and in the polity of a church that allowed for a considerable diversity of belief among its communicants. Beset with all the

---

3 Hebrew for 'devastation' and therefore an increasingly preferred word for the Nazi atrocities against the Jews than the Greek 'Holocaust', which means 'sacrifice' or 'offering' and implies a redemptive purpose.

4 Thomas Cranmer, *The Remains of Thomas Cranmer*, 4 vols, ed. Henry Jenkins (Oxford: Oxford University Press, 1833), vol. 2, p. 157.

characteristic debates and disputes of the twenty-first century, experiencing the reality of division and sectarianism, the Anglican Communion has never more needed to reclaim this spiritual birthright from its founder.

He might offer something, too, to the conduct of public office. Cranmer's willingness to compromise, his shrewd sense of when a situation was hopeless and when it could be influenced, and even his capacity to show real, iron courage in both contexts, have often been held up for criticism. In fact, they also demonstrate an astute grasp of reality and an enviable sense of his own agency and its limitations. Three hundred years before it was written, Cranmer lived by Reinhold Niebuhr's 'serenity' prayer:

> God, give us grace to accept with serenity
> the things that cannot be changed,
> Courage to change the things
> which should be changed,
> and the Wisdom to distinguish
> the one from the other.

While some excoriate him for failing to save Thomas More (who could not have been saved) or for his collaboration in the dismissal of Queen Catherine, we should remember too that he pleaded for Anne Boleyn's innocence with an angry king long after her fate was sealed; he lived faithfully and devotedly for 15 years with a wife and family whom the law forbade him to acknowledge; he vigorously fought his case with King and Council when he felt able to steer them towards further reform; he implemented a root-and-branch renewal of Christianity in England with great zeal and impressive authority; and he stood unrepentantly and increasingly alone against the early moves of Queen Mary and her Council. Moreover, he died with a dignity which it is given to few to possess, conscious predominantly only of his own failings. These are qualities sorely needed in our public life, in which compromise is largely despised and courage lacking, and standing against the mainstream of one's party or group an act considered treacherous. Even amid the polarized atmosphere of sixteenth-century religion and the Tudor court, Cranmer offers us pause for reflection.

Archbishop Cranmer's long career exemplifies also the virtues of tenacity and humility. He was a man able to acknowledge the ways in which his views changed, and able to express gratitude for finding himself questioning the assumptions and certainties of his youth. Not a man in this area for political sleight of hand or attempts to cover over his own development, he shows us that it is possible honourably to grow and renew oneself, even indeed while holding high office. The intentional gradualism of his reforms to English Christianity reflects both an intuitive grasp of the English (perhaps just human!) character and its slowness to embrace and adapt to change, and his deep, visceral and yet realistic, commitment to his task, to ensuring that services were in English, that congregants could participate in the Communion fully, that economic grievances were addressed, and that piety could benefit the lives of all, rich and poor. Once he had set his hand to the plough, Thomas Cranmer rarely looked back and, more remarkably, rarely lamented his lot. He was that rarest of phenomena: a wielder of real power who viewed his life's purpose, not as seeking greater preferment or wealth or merely personal influence but as securing the advancement of what he understood to be truth in the realm. Modern management theory these days has developed a language of 'servant leadership'. While it is something highly to be commended, it can be sometimes superficial or ill-informed and occasionally even a cynical veneer placed on the same old authoritarian or exploitative practices. A life like Cranmer's, in which the long exercise of high office is used consistently to advocate for the greater inclusion of ordinary people and the improvement of their situation, is still a stirring challenge to our faddishness, reminding us to make good on our slogans and to be honourable in our intentions.

Above all these qualities and virtues, and despite all his faults and failings, Cranmer's greatest achievement will always be in the use of language. No-one has ever written prayers like him; no-one has either ever had a better grasp of the flow and beauty of a good liturgy or more presciently understood what enables the expression of corporate spirituality. No-one has ever eclipsed him either in shaping the vocabulary of the English-speaking world, save perhaps Shakespeare. The myriad daily acts of Christian worship which still use his prose, and the countless ways in which his compositions and translations influence our speech are his supreme monument. Using the form he perfected, a contemporary collect composed in honour of the Archbishop and in praise of his God should have the last word:

Everlasting God, your servant Thomas Cranmer restored the language of the people in the prayers of the Church. Make us always thankful for his heritage and help us so to pray in the Spirit and with the understanding, that we may worthily magnify your holy Name; through Jesus Christ our Lord. Amen.[5]

---

5 *Celebrating Common Prayer* (London: Mowbray, 1992), p. 440.

Appendix

The Forty-Two Articles, 1553

These articles of faith, drawing for their model on the much shorter sets of articles issued under Henry VIII, were promulgated early in 1553, just when Edward VI began to show the symptoms of the disease that would soon kill him. Cranmer was urgently requiring clergy to subscribe to them, even as he was summoned to sign the papers that tried to make Jane Grey queen. The articles were thus a dead letter almost as soon as they were produced, but survive as a clear snapshot of how decidedly Reformed in character the Church in England had become. Under Elizabeth I, they became the foundation of the reduced[1] Thirty-Nine Articles of 1563, which remain one of the central theological definitions of Anglicanism.

Articles agreed on by the Bishops, and other learned men in the Synod at London, in the year of our Lord 1552, for the avoiding of controversy in opinions, and the establishment of a godly concord, in certain matters of Religion.[2]

1. Of faith in the holy Trinity
There is but one living and true God, and he is everlasting without body, parts or passions, of infinite power, wisdom and goodness, the maker, and preserver of all things both visible, and invisible, and in unity of this Godhead there be three persons of one substance, power, and eternity, the Father, the Son and the holy Ghost.

2. That the word, or Son of God, was made a very man
The son which is the word of the Father, took man's nature in the womb of the blessed virgin Mary of her Substance, so that two

---

1 The altered or omitted articles were mostly to do with eucharistic theology, edging the English Church gently in a more 'Lutheran' direction.

2 This claim was in fact untrue. The full Convocation of clergy had not agreed the Articles, and Cranmer was angry at the mistake in the title-page, which had been printed by the Council without his involvement.

whole, and perfect natures, that is to say, the Godhead, and manhood were joined together into one person, never to be divided, whereof is one Christ, very God, and very man, who truly suffered, was crucified, dead, and buried, to reconcile his father to us, and to be a Sacrifice for all sin of man, both original and actual.

3. Of the going down of Christ into Hell
As Christ died, and was buried for us: so also it is to be believed, that he went down into hell. For the body lay in the Sepulchre, until the resurrection: but his Ghost departing from him, was with the Ghosts that were in prison, or in Hell, and did preach to the same, as the place of St. Peter doth testify.

4. The Resurrection of Christ
Christ did truly rise again from death, and took again his body with flesh, bones, and all things appertaining to the perfection of man's nature, wherewith he ascended into Heaven, and there sitteth, until he return to judge men at the last day.

5. The doctrine of holy Scripture is sufficient to Salvation
Holy Scripture containeth all things necessary to Salvation: so that whatsoever is neither read therein, nor may be proved thereby, although it be sometime received of the faithful, as Godly, and profitable for an order, and comeliness: Yet no man ought to be constrained to believe it as an article of faith, or repute it requisite to the necessity of Salvation.

6. The Old Testament is not to be refused
The old Testament is not to be put away as though it were contrary to the new, but to be kept still: for both in the old, and new Testaments, everlasting life is offered to mankind by Christ, who is the only mediator between God, and man, being both God, and man. Wherefore they are not to be heard, which feign that old Fathers did look only for transitory promises.

7. The three Creeds
The three Creeds, Nicene Creed, Athanasius' Creed, and that which is commonly called the Apostles' Creed, ought thoroughly to be received: for they may be proved by most certain warranties of holy Scripture.

8. Of original, or birth sin

Original Sin standeth not in the following of Adam, as the Pelagians do vainly talk, which also the Anabaptists do nowadays renew, but it is the fault, and corruption of the nature of every man that naturally is engendered by the offspring of Adam, whereby man is very far gone from his former righteousness which he had at his creation and is of his own nature given to evil, so that the flesh desireth always contrary to the spirit, and therefore in every person born into this world, it deserveth God's wrath and damnation: And this infection of nature doth remain, yea in them that are baptized, whereby the lust of the flesh called in Greek φρονημα σαρκος (which some do expound, the Wisdom, some sensuality, some the affection, some the desire of the flesh) is not subject to the law of God. And although there is no condemnation for them that believe, and are baptized, yet the Apostle doth confess, that concupiscence, and lust hath of itself the nature of sin.[3]

9. Of free will

We have no power to do good works pleasant, and acceptable to God, without the Grace of God by Christ, preventing us that we may have a good will, and work in us, when we have that will.

10. Of Grace

The Grace of Christ, or the holy Ghost by him given doth take away the stony heart, and giveth an heart of flesh. And although, those that have no will to good things, he maketh them to will the same: Yet nevertheless he enforceth not the will. And therefore no man when he sinneth, can excuse himself, as not worthy to be blamed, or condemned, by alleging that he sinned unwillingly, or by compulsion.

---

3 The articles deal with ancient theological debate here. The Pelagians were those who placed great emphasis on human effort and will in the quest for holiness, distrusting the idea of original sin, and against whom Augustine of Hippo devoted much ink and literary venom. The Anabaptists represented the extreme of Reformation thought (believing among other things in baptism for adult believers only) and similarly found themselves the target of both Protestant and Catholic vitriol. 'Concupiscence' is Augustine's idea, renewed by Luther and others, that sexual intercourse itself passes on Adam's innate sinfulness from generation to generation.

11. Of the Justification of man
Justification by only faith in Jesus Christ in that sense, as it is declared in the homily of Justification,[4] is a most certain, and wholesome doctrine for Christian men.

12. Works before Justification
Works done before the Grace of Christ and the inspiration of his spirit are not pleasant to God, forasmuch as they spring not of Faith in Jesus Christ, neither do they make men to receive Grace, or as the School authorities say, deserve Grace of congruity: but because they are not done as God hath willed, and commanded them to be done, we doubt not but they have the nature of sin.

13. Works of Supererogation
Voluntary works besides, over, and above God's commandments, which they call works of Supererogation, cannot be taught without arrogancy, and iniquity. For by them men do declare, that they do not only render to God, as much as they are bound to do, but that they do more for his sake, than of bounden duty is required: Whereas Christ saith plainly: when you have done all that are commanded you, say, we be unprofitable servants.

14. No man is without sin, but Christ alone
Christ in the truth of our nature was made like unto us in all things, sin only except, from which he was clearly void both in his Flesh, and in his Spirit. He came to be the lamb without spot, who by Sacrifice of himself made once forever, should take away the sins of the world: and sin (as Saint John saith) was not in him. But the rest, yea, although we be baptized, and born again in Christ, yet we all offend in many things: and if we say, we have no Sin, we deceive ourselves, and the truth is not in us.

15. Of sin against the holy Ghost
Every deadly sin willingly committed after Baptism, is not Sin against the holy Ghost, and unpardonable: wherefore the place for penance, is not to be denied to such as fall into sin after Baptism. After we have received the holy Ghost, we may depart from grace given, and fall into sin, and by the grace of God we may rise again, and amend

---

4 See above, Chapter 3. Cranmer must have taken particular pleasure in this article, after his troubles persuading Henry VIII to embrace this idea.

our lives. And therefore they are to be condemned, which say, they can no more sin as long as they live here, or deny the place for penitence to such as truly repent, and amend their lives.

16. Blasphemy against the holy Ghost
Blasphemy against the holy Ghost is, when a man of malice, and stubbornness of mind doth rail upon the truth of God's word manifestly perceived, and being enemy thereunto persecuteth the same. And because such be guilty of God's curse, they entangle themselves with a most grievous, and heinous crime, whereupon this kind of sin is called, and affirmed of the Lord, unpardonable.

17. Of predestination, and Election
Predestination to life, is the everlasting purpose of God, whereby (before the foundations of the world were laid) he hath constantly decreed by his own Judgement secret to us, to deliver from curse, and damnation those whom he hath chosen out of mankind, and to bring them to everlasting salvation by Christ, as vessels made to honour: whereupon, such as have so excellent a benefit of God given unto them be called, according to God's purpose, by his spirit working in due season, they through grace obey the calling, they be justified freely, they be made sons by adoption, they be made like the image of God's only begotten son Jesus Christ, they walk religiously in good works, and at length by God's mercy, they attain to everlasting felicity.

As the godly consideration of Predestination, and our election in Christ is full of sweet, pleasant, and unspeakable comfort to godly persons, and such as feel in themselves the working of the spirit of Christ, mortifying the works of the flesh, and their earthly members, and drawing up their mind to high, and heavenly things, as well because it doth greatly stablish and confirm their faith of eternal Salvation to be enjoined through Christ, as because it doth fervently kindle their love towards God: So for curious, and carnal persons lacking the spirit of Christ, to have continually before their eyes the sentence of God's predestination, is a most dangerous downfall, whereby the Devil may thrust them either into desperation, or into a recklessness of most unclean living, no less perilous than desperation.

Furthermore, although the Decrees of predestination are unknown to us, yet we must receive God's promises, in such wise as they be generally set forth to us in holy Scripture, and in our doings that will of God is to be followed, which we have expressly declared unto us in the word of God.

18. We must trust to obtain eternal Salvation only by the name of Christ

They also are to be had accursed, and abhorred that presume to say, that every man shall be saved by the Law, or sect which he professeth, so that he be diligent to frame his life according to that Law, and the light of Nature: for holy Scripture doth set unto us only the name of Jesus Christ whereby men must be saved.

19. All men are bound to keep the moral commandments of the Law

The Law, which was given of God by Moses, although it bind not Christian men, as concerning the Ceremonies, and Rites of the same: Neither is it required that the Civil Precepts, and Orders of it should of necessity be received in any common weal: yet no man, be he never so perfect a Christian, is exempt, and loose from the Obedience of those Commandments, which are called Moral: wherefore they are not to be harkened unto, who affirm that holy Scripture is given only to the weak, and do boast themselves continually of the spirit of whom (they say) they have learned such things, as they teach, although the same be most evidently repugnant to the holy Scripture.

20. Of the Church

The visible Church of Christ is a Congregation of faithful Men, in the which the pure word of God is preached, and the sacraments be duly ministered, according to Christ's ordinance, in all those things that of necessity are requisite to the same.

As the Church of Jerusalem, of Alexandria, and of Antioch hath erred: So also the Church of Rome hath erred not only in their living, but also in matters of their faith.

21. Of the authority of the Church

It is not lawful for the Church to ordain anything that is contrary to God's word written, neither may it so expound one place of scripture, that it be repugnant to another. Wherefore although the Church be a witness and a keeper of holy writ, yet as it ought not to decree anything against the same: So besides the same, ought it not to enforce anything to be believed for necessity of Salvation.

22. Of the authority of general Councils

General councils may not be gathered together, without the commandment, and will of Princes: and when they be gathered (forasmuch as they be an assembly of men whereof all be not governed with the spirit, and word of God) they may err, and sometimes have erred, not only in worldly matters, but also in things pertaining unto God. Wherefore things ordained by them, as necessary to Salvation, have neither strength, nor authority, unless it may be declared, that they be taken out of holy Scripture.

23. Of Purgatory
The doctrine of School authors concerning purgatory, Pardons, Worshipping, and adoration as well of Images as of relics, and also invocation of Saints, is a fond thing vainly feigned, and grounded upon no warrant of scripture, but rather repugnant to the word of God.

24. No man may minister in the Congregation, except he be called
It is not lawful for any man to take upon him the office of Public preaching, or ministering the sacraments in the congregation, before he be lawfully called, and sent to execute the same. And those we ought to judge lawfully called, and sent, which be chosen, and called to this work by men, who have public authority given unto them in the congregation, to call, and send ministers into the Lord's vineyard.

25. Men must speak in the Congregation in such tongue as the people understandeth
It is most seemly, and most agreeable to the word of God, that in the congregation nothing be openly read, or spoken in a tongue unknown to the people, the which thing St. Paul did forbid, except some were present that should declare the same.

26. Of the Sacraments
Our Lord Jesus Christ hath knit together a company of new people with Sacraments, most few in number, most easy to be kept, most excellent in signification, as is Baptism, and the Lord's Supper.

The Sacraments were not ordained of Christ to be gazed upon, or to be carried about, but that we should rightly use them. And in such only, as worthily receive the same, they have an wholesome effect, and operation, and yet not that of the work wrought, as some men speak, which word, as it is strange, and unknown to holy Scripture: So it engendereth no Godly, but a very superstitious sense. But they that receive the Sacraments unworthily, purchase to themselves Damnation, as St. Paul saith.

Sacraments ordained by the Word of God be not only Badges, and tokens of Christian men's profession, but rather they be certain sure witnesses, and effectual signs of grace, and God's good will toward us, by the which he doth work invisible in us, and doth not only quicken, but also strengthen, and confirm our faith in him.

27. The wickedness of the Ministers doth not take away the effectual operation of God's ordinances

Although in the visible Church the evil be ever mingled with the good, and sometime the evil have chief authority in the ministration of the word, and Sacraments: yet forasmuch as they do not the same in their own name, but do minister by Christ's commission, and authority: we may use their ministry both in hearing the word of God, and in the receiving the sacraments, neither is the effect of God's Ordinances taken away by their Wickedness, or the grace of God's gift diminished from such, as by faith, and rightly receive the Sacraments ministered unto them, which be effectual, because of Christ's institution, and promise, although they be ministered by evil men. Nevertheless it appertaineth to the discipline of the Church, that enquiry be made of such, and that they be accused by those that have knowledge of their offences, and finally being found guilty by just judgement be deposed.

28. Of Baptism

Baptism is not only a sign of profession, and mark of difference, whereby Christian men are discerned from other that be not Christened, but it is also a sign, and seal of our new birth, whereby, as by an instrument they that receive Baptism rightly, are grafted in the Church, the promises of forgiveness of Sin, and our Adoption to be the sons of God, are visibly signed and sealed, faith is confirmed, and grace increased by virtue of prayer unto God. The custom of the Church to Christen young children, is to be commended, and in any wise to be retained in the Church.

29. Of the Lord's Supper

The Supper of the Lord is not only a sign of the love that Christians ought to have among themselves one to another, but rather it is a sacrament of our redemption by Christ's death, insomuch that to such as rightly, worthily, and with faith receive the same, the bread which we break, is a communion of the body of Christ. Likewise, the Cup of blessing, is a Communion of the blood of Christ.

Transubstantiation, or the change of the substance of bread and wine into the substance of Christ's body, and blood cannot be proved by holy writ, but is repugnant to the plain words of Scripture, and hath given occasion to many superstitions.

Forasmuch as the truth of man's nature requireth, that the body of one, and the selfsame man cannot be at one time in diverse places, but must needs be in some one certain place: Therefore the body of Christ cannot be present at one time in many and diverse places. And because (as holy Scripture doth teach) Christ was taken up into heaven, and there shall continue unto the end of the world, a faithful man ought not, either to believe or openly to confess the real and bodily presence (as they term it) of Christ's flesh and blood in the Sacrament of the Lord's Supper.

The Sacrament of the Lord's Supper was not commanded by Christ's ordinance to be kept, carried about, lifted up, nor worshipped.

30. Of the perfect oblation of Christ made upon the cross
The offering of Christ made once forever, is the perfect redemption, the pacifying of God's displeasure, and satisfaction for all the sins of the whole world, both original and actual: and there is none other satisfaction for sin, but that alone. Wherefore the sacrifices of masses in the which it was commonly said, that the Priest did offer Christ for the quick, and the dead, to have remission of pain or sin, were forged fables, and dangerous deceits.

31. The state of single life is commanded to no man by the word of God
Bishops, Priests, and Deacons are not commanded to vow the state of single life without marriage, neither by God's law are they compelled to abstain from matrimony.

32. Excommunicate persons are to be avoided
That person, which by open denunciation of the Church, is rightly cut off from the unity of the Church, and excommunicate, ought to be taken of the whole multitude of the faithful, as an Heathen, an publican, until he be openly reconciled by penance, and received into the Church by a Judge that hath authority thereto.

33. Traditions of the Church
It is not necessary that traditions and ceremonies be in all places one, or utterly like. For at all times they have been diverse, and may be

changed, according to the diversity of countries, and men's manners, so that nothing be ordained against God's word.

Whosoever through his private judgement willingly, and purposely doth openly break the traditions and Ceremonies of the Church, which be not repugnant to the word of God, and be ordained, and approved by common authority, ought to be rebuked openly (that other may fear to do the like) as one that offendeth against the common order of the church, and hurteth the authority of the Magistrate, and woundeth the consciences of the weak brethren.

34. Homilies
The Homilies of late given, and set out by the King's authority, be godly and wholesome, containing doctrine to be received of all men, and therefore are to be read to the people diligently, distinctly, and plainly.

35. Of the book of Prayers, and Ceremonies of the Church of England
The Book which of very late time was given to the Church of England by the King's authority, and the Parliament, containing the manner and form of praying, and ministering the Sacraments in the Church of England, likewise also the book of ordering Ministers of the Church, set forth by the foresaid authority, are godly, and in no point repugnant to the wholesome doctrine of the Gospel but agreeable thereunto, furthering and beautifying the same not a little, and therefore of all faithful members of the Church of England, and chiefly of the Ministers of the word, they ought to be received and allowed with all readiness of mind, and thanksgiving, and to be commended to the people of God.

36. Of Civil magistrates
The King of England is Supreme head in earth, next under Christ, of the Church of England, and Ireland.

The Bishop of Rome hath no jurisdiction in this Realm of England.

The civil Magistrate is ordained, and allowed of God: wherefore we must obey him, not only for fear of punishment, but also for conscience's sake.

The civil laws may punish Christian men with death, for heinous, and grievous offences.

It is lawful for Christians, at the commandment of the Magistrate, to wear weapons, and to serve in lawful wars.

37. Christian men's goods are not commune (communal, held in common)

The riches and goods of Christians are not communal as touching the right title and possession of the same (as certain anabaptists do falsely boast) notwithstanding every man ought of such things as he possesseth liberally to give alms to the poor, according to his ability.

38. Christian men may take an Oath

As we confess that vain, and rash swearing is forbidden Christian men by our Lord Jesus Christ, and his Apostle James: so we judge that Christian religion doth not prohibit, but that a man may swear, when the magistrate requireth in a cause of faith and charity, so it be done (according to the Prophet's teaching) in justice, judgement, and truth.

39. The Resurrection of the dead is not yet brought to pass

The Resurrection of the dead is not as yet brought to pass, as though it only belonged to the soul, which by the grace of Christ is raised from the death of sin, but it is to be looked for at the last day: for then (as Scripture doth most manifestly testify) to all that be dead their own bodies, flesh and bone shall be restored, that the whole man may (according to his works) have other reward, or punishment, as he hath lived virtuously, or wickedly.

40. The souls of them that depart this life neither die with the bodies, nor sleep idly

They which say, that the souls of such as depart hence do sleep, being without all sense, feeling, or perceiving, until the day of judgement, or affirm that the souls die with the bodies, and at the last day shall be raised up with the same, do utterly dissent from the right belief declared to us in holy Scripture.

41. Heretics called Millenarii[5]

They that go about to renew the fable of heretics called Millenarii, be repugnant to holy Scripture, and cast themselves headlong into a Jewish dotage.

---

5 The sixteenth century had its share of bizarre apocalyptic sects, just as does the twenty-first.

42. All men shall not be saved at the length

They also are worthy of condemnation who endeavour at this time to restore the dangerous opinion, that all men, be they never so ungodly, shall at length be saved, when they have suffered pains for their sins a certain time appointed by God's justice.

God save the King.

Some Further Reading

Brooks, Peter Newman, *Thomas Cranmer's Doctrine of the Eucharist* (London: Macmillan, 1992).

Cameron, Euan, *The European Reformation* (Oxford: Oxford University Press, 1991).

Cranmer, Thomas, *The Remains of Thomas Cranmer*, 4 vols, ed. Henry Jenkins (Oxford: Oxford University Press, 1833).

Cranmer, Thomas, *The works of Thomas Cranmer, Archbishop of Canterbury, Martyr 1556*, 2 vols, ed. John Edmund Cox (Cambridge: Parker Society, 1844–6), vol. 1, *Writings and disputations, relative to the sacrament of the Lord's Supper*; vol. 2, *Miscellaneous writings and letters*.

Duffy, Eamon, *Fires of Faith: Catholic England under Mary Tudor* (New Haven and London: Yale University Press, 2009).

Duffy, Eamon, *The Stripping of the Altars* (New Haven and London: Yale University Press, 1992).

Haigh, Christopher, *English Reformations* (Oxford: Oxford University Press, 1993).

Hefling, Charles, and Cynthia Shattuck (eds), *The Oxford Guide to the Book of Common Prayer* (Oxford: Oxford University Press, 2006).

Loades, David, *Mary Tudor* (Oxford: Blackwell, 1989).

Loades, David, *The Reign of Mary Tudor* (London and New York: Longman, 1991).

MacCulloch, Diarmaid, *Thomas Cranmer* (New Haven and London: Yale University Press, 1996).

MacCulloch, Diarmaid, *Tudor Church Militant* (London: Penguin, 1999).

Marshall, Peter, and Alec Ryrie (eds), *The Beginnings of English Protestantism* (Cambridge: Cambridge University Press, 2002).

Procter, Francis, and Walter Howard Frere, *A New History of the Book of Common Prayer* (London: Macmillan, 1941).

Scarisbrick, Jack, *Henry VIII* (London: Eyre and Spottiswood, 1968).

CPSIA information can be obtained at www.ICGtesting.com
Printed in the USA
LVOW081613170812

294736LV00002B/4/P

9 781848 250482